Rainhouse & Ocean

Ruth M. Underhill

Donald M. Bahr

Baptisto Lopez

Jose Pancho

David Lopez

Rainhouse & Ocean

Speeches for the Papago Year

THE UNIVERSITY OF ARIZONA PRESS TUCSON

Since this volume was first issued in 1979, the Arizona people formerly known as Papago Indians have officially changed their name to Tohono O'odham (Desert People). The change was adopted as part of a new constitution approved by members of the Tohono O'odham Nation (formerly the Papago Indian Tribe of Arizona) in January 1986.

First University of Arizona Press paperbound edition published 1997 by arrangement with the Museum of Northern Arizona.

Library of Congress Cataloging-in-Publication Data
Rainhouse and ocean : speeches for the Papago year /
Ruth M. Underhill . . . [et al.].
p. cm.
English and Papago.
Originally published: [Flagstaff] : Museum of Northern Arizona Press, c1979.
Includes bibliographical references (p.) and index.
ISBN 0-8165-1774-6 (paper : alk. paper)
1. Tohono O'odham Indians—Rites and ceremonies. 2. Speeches, addresses, etc., Tohono O'odham. I. Underhill, Ruth Murray, 1884–1984.
E99.P25R3 1997
299'.74–dc21 96-52169

Manufactured in the United States of America on acid-free, archival-quality paper.

12 11 10 09 08 07 7 6 5 4 3 2

Contents

ILLUSTRATIONS

Illustrations continued

Introduction

On a map of the southwestern United States, one sees Arizona and New Mexico edged with a jagged black line which goes from Texas to the Pacific. This is the Mexican border. It seems an unlikely place for defining territory. There is no stream to cross, no mountain ridge to prevent progress. Indians, in fact, may have wandered across it for hundreds of years without restriction. Then two growing republics, Mexico and the United States, laid down their line of separation (in 1853). This meant that for thousands of Indians their whole lifeway would in time be changed. Without being consulted, they would find themselves adopting different houses, clothing and food, different languages, and, eventually a different religion.

Among these were the Papagos. They and their relatives, the Pima, were members of a great language group which students have called "Uto-Aztecan." It included the Utes of Utah, various California tribes which are now almost forgotten, the Hopi of Arizona, and the Aztecs of Mexico. All these in the course of history had developed different customs and slightly different languages. However, the Papago have retained one Mexican ceremony which speaks clearly of the south as no other. This is the *Navait*, to be described below.

I came to the Papago in 1931. Students in the States were interested to know how the change of citizenship from Mexican to American was affecting the Papago. They took it calm and smiling, as they took everything. Most of them spoke some Spanish and perhaps a little English. They had wandered about the country near the reservation for years selling their pots or taking day work. Their men had helped the United States Army on some occasions.

The Papagos were still new citizens of the United States, for their reservation had been set up only in 1917. A brand new headquarters called Sells had been established there. It had modern buildings with wooden floors and running water. There was a superintendent with clerks and an elementary day school.

This was for children. The adults were expected to learn English for themselves, even in the difficult matter of dollars and cents, pounds and quarts. Three villages also had elementary day schools. The Catholics had seven schools and a number of churches.

The villagers, beside their yearly trek to Magdalena for Catholic ceremonies established long ago, also built small churches of their own. For these, there was generally no priest but some devout woman who had learned at least the Rosary and could recite to a congregation of her relatives The two religions and two life-ways seemed to jog along comfortably together, each fulfilling a need without disturbing the other.

My first season with the Papago was spent mostly with women. Men, I decided, might look askance at a lone female asking to talk with them on ceremony, which was their principal subject. In fact I was right, for the Papago made strong distinction in the occupations of the sexes. Men did the farming and tended to the horses. Women gathered wild plants for food and basketry. All played games, which included gambling and racing; but men played with men and women with women. There was a difference even in their language, at least in relationship terms. Father and mother addressed their children in different ways, and the children reciprocated. So I had plenty to do in learning to speak Papago as a female should. This included leaving out "r" and "f" in favor of "l" and "p." It also included taking little breaths at the beginning and end of a word. I worked at it and was highly pleased when the children told me I had a nickname —"Plain Speaker."

"Dear me," I thought, "I must be getting on well with learning Papago!" That satisfaction did not last when I heard the next woman speak.

I attended all the ceremonies with my women friends and listened carefully to the male ceremonialists. They had at least three ways of speaking. First was the usual way in an everyday voice. This was for welcoming guests and telling the news. Then came a custom which was called, "Throwing Words." It meant that each word came out separately, with great emphasis and in a loud voice. It was meant for an audience on a special occasion, but not for the spirits. I found the same custom later among the Mohave. The third manner of speaking was one described in this paper. It concerned sacred subjects and was often meant to be heard not by an audience, but by the spirits who were thus reminded of their obligations.

Finally, the "Plain Speaker" felt that the time had come when she must venture contact with the men and attempt to write down some of the ceremonies.

"We can't help you," the women said. "We know the stories behind the ceremonies but not the songs which make them powerful. For those you must go to the old men." This meant, I found, the hereditary specialists, each of whom had learned his speeches from a male ancestor. But the speeches were not in modern Papago, and I might even have difficulty in getting the words.

I inquired around the reservation for an interpreter, but that was no simple matter. Some men could explain the ceremonies to me in Spanish but not in English. The words they knew in my native language were usually not dignified ones, and the school, which did teach long words out of books and out of the Bible, was only for children. Finally, I heard of Juan Xavier. His name is spelled by my coauthors with an "H" as the Anglos might write it. Juan preferred to use the Spanish spelling as was done by the great missionary, Saint Francis Xavier. This he learned when he went away to school. The reservation had no high school in those early days, and one who wanted an education had to search for it. The only opportunity Juan found was the Cook Bible School in Phoenix. Young Indians of various southwestern tribes could learn English there in connection with their religious education in Presbyterian theology. If they finished the course, they were sent out among their tribesmen to teach the Gospel as seen by the Anglos. The People received this version of Christianity as they had received the Spanish priests years ago. This did not mean giving up their own ceremonies. They simply took the new ones in addition, perhaps feeling that all spirit power must be welcome. Juan, when I met him, was no longer preaching. I heard of his eloquence at outlying government stations where I visited, but he had felt the need of earning money. He had had various jobs but when I met him was looking for a new one. He was more than delighted to speak English with me and to work out interpretations for the ancient ceremonies.

I hesitated to go to the old ceremonialists myself to explain why I wished to understand their ritual. The reason was so that these could be written down and used by Papagos for many years to come. The old priests were dying, and some had not taught their ceremonials to younger men. If this continued, the beautiful language and all the actions connected with it might be lost. I explained all this to Juan and found him very enthusiastic. He, too, wanted a clearer understanding of the ceremonies; but he had been away and had made no connections which would help him to learn about them. So he and I held conferences where we went over the subject carefully. I told him what I wanted to say to the respected speechmakers and why. I told him that the words must be written down in Papago just as they had always been said. Still, I wanted them translated into English so that the Anglo officials and school teachers could understand them. Juan was amazed and delighted that such a thing could be done. He made an eager and reverent ambassador, arranging appointments for me with one ceremonialist after the other. The men, by this time, knew who I was. Their women had recommended me as humble and willing to learn. I had, indeed, a horn phonograph with which I later took some songs. For the speeches, I had to use the recommendation given me by my phonetics teacher at Columbia: "Just wash your ears out."

I wrote down the speeches in pencil in a stenographer's notebook, and a slow performance it was. Each ceremonialist, in the first place, spoke slowly and with long pauses for thought. I had been trained using the phonetic alphabet to represent any sound. When I read to the dictator what I had written he did not criticize me for a fault I learned of later, that is, giving a soft sound of a consonant instead of the hard one—"p" for "b," "t" for "d." Having written, I thought, exactly what the speaker said, Juan would go over it with him; and he would explain the meaning as it was in his time. That I would write, and under it the meaning which Juan gave at present—that is, if he knew of a meaning. Then came the problem of putting the whole into readable English. I have been told that my result sounded like the Psalms, but why not? These were poetic descriptions of a ceremony held by farming people whose life was not too unlike

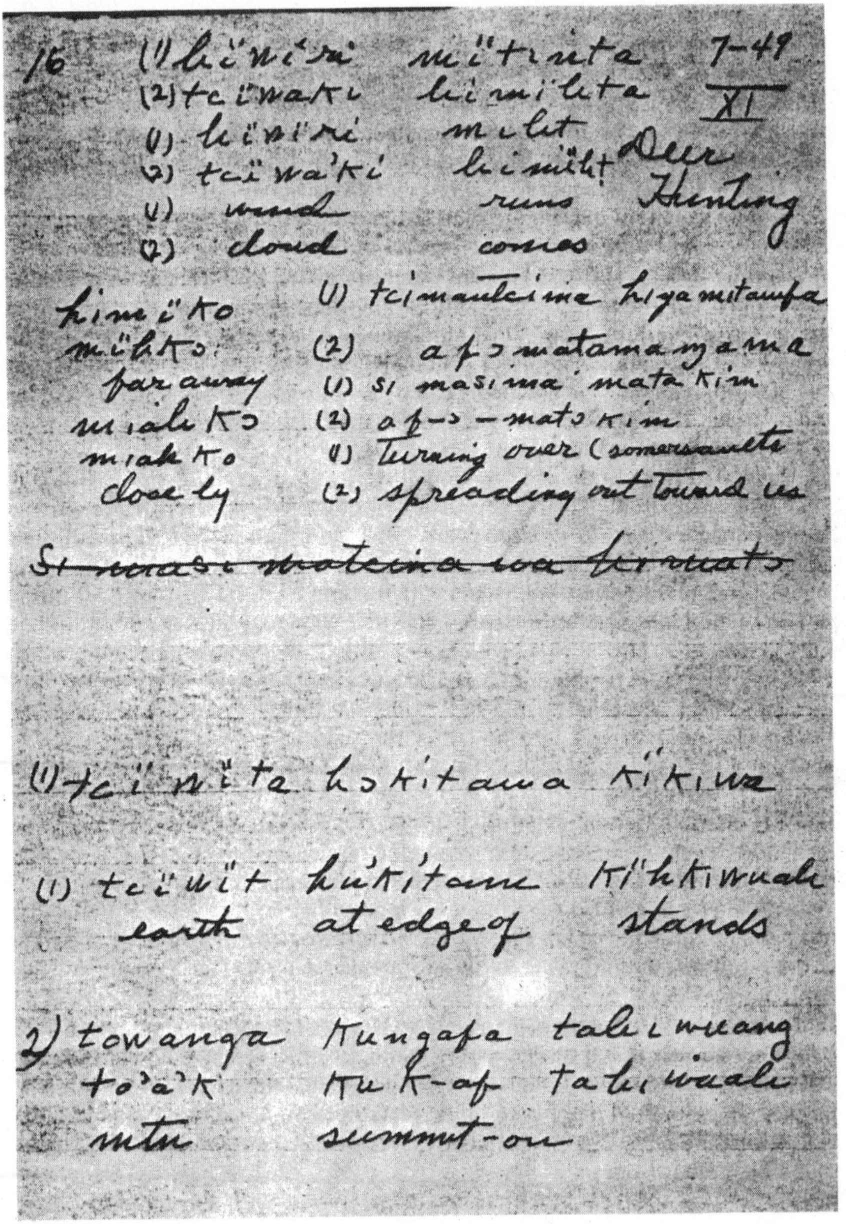

16 (1) hïwïri mïtinta 7-49
(2) tcïwaki himilita XI
(1) hïwïri milit Deer
(2) tcïwaki himilit Hunting
(1) wind runs
(2) cloud comes

himeïko (1) tcimantcima hiyamitanfa
mïhko (2) afomatamamyama
far away (1) si masima matakim
mialiko (2) af-o-matokim
miakko (1) turning over (somersaults
closely (2) spreading out toward us

~~Si masi matcima wa kiroats~~

(1) tcïmita hokitama kikiwa

(1) tcïwit hukitam kihkiwuali
earth at edge of stands

2) towanga kungafa taliwuang
toa'k kuk-af taliwuali
mtn summit-on

A page of Ruth M. Underhill's notebook, showing her method of transcription and translation.

that of the ancient Hebrews. In those hot days, I had had to borrow a towel from the housewife to put under my arm as it rested on the arm of a camp chair. Otherwise, the perspiration would have soaked the pencil writing.

So in partnership between Xavier and Underhill was written out a first English version of some very ancient Uto-Aztecan ceremonies. It may seem unnatural to present-day Papagos as well as incorrect. Perhaps as time goes on and interest in old customs grows among all of us, it may be worthwhile to consult these first attempts at transcribing the sacred ceremonies of the northern Papago.[1]

Ruth M. Underhill
July 1979
Denver Colo.

PURPOSE OF THIS BOOK

This book describes one side of the yearly ritual cycle of the Papago Indians of southern Arizona and northern Sonora, Mexico—the Native as opposed to the Christian side. Seven rites will be treated in turn to show how they form a whole system of meanings. It is a system that grew from the relation between the Papagos and their desert homeland. In its details it could belong to no other people as, for example, the rains which are very important in this system come from a certain direction at a certain time of year, the ocean which is also quite important lies in a different direction, etc. We will see how thoroughly the old time ritualists knew their world.

The book is written with two groups of readers in mind. The first group is Papagos who may know more or less about their native ritual tradition. The writers hope that young Papagos in the year 2000 will find this book informative and that old Papagos of today will find it truthful. The second group is the general public. It is hoped that readers interested in religion, arid lands, poetry, and Indian cultures—singly or in combination—will find the book of value.

We will concentrate on a type of text which should challenge the most expert Papago or member of the general public. These are texts of the speeches used in each rite. One cannot understand the ritual year without reference to these texts, just as one cannot understand a university without reference to its books, or a religion without reference to its liturgy. But only a very expert Papago would understand the texts without considerable additional background on the rites.

[1]Ruth Underhill's original transcriptions and translations are stored in the Archives of the Denver Museum of Natural History Department of Anthropology, Denver, Colorado.

Editor's Note: Ruth Underhill emphasizes that her responsibility in this book is limited to the above portion of the Introduction and to having supplied the original texts (see footnote 2, page 7). Her own descriptions of Papago government and religion may be found in *Social Organization of the Papago Indians*, 1939 and in *Papago Religion*, 1946. She does not necessarily subscribe to the interpretations contained in the body of this book.

MAP

of the Papago Reservations
showing villages from which speeches were obtained

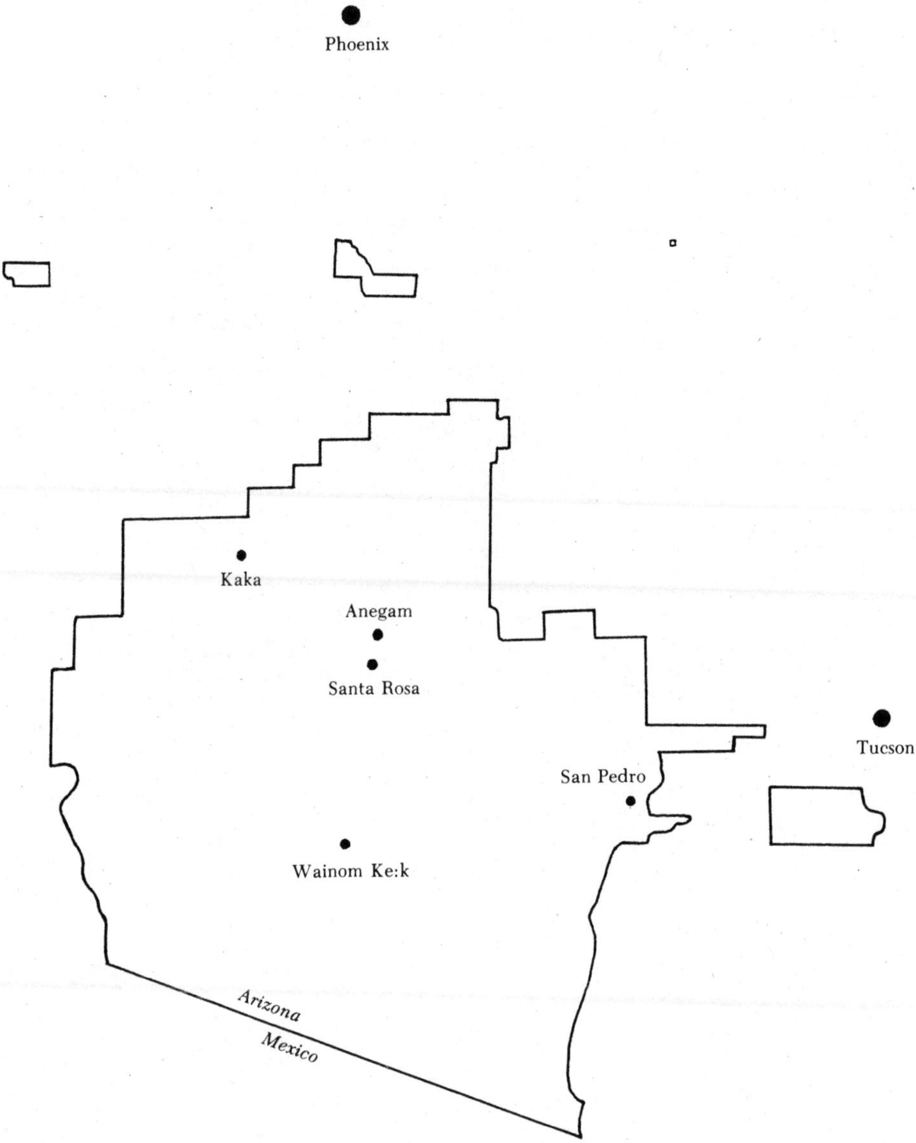

Two such experts are among the coauthors,[2] to aid in the practical task of the book, which is to explain the ritual year by means of the texts and to explain the texts by means of the ritual year.

PAPAGO RELIGION AS A WHOLE

The Papagos live on a reservation the size of a small state along the Mexican border of Arizona. They have four smaller reservations in the same general territory, and there are some Papago villages just over the border in Mexico. They speak dialects of one basic language, "Piman" or "Pima-Papago." (The closely related Pimas speak the same language and have their own set of reservations in Arizona.) The speakers of each dialect have their own traditions going back for hundreds of years, but there is reason to believe that these traditions are variations of one basic culture. Perhaps the best reason for believing this is that when a speaker of one dialect goes far enough back in his history of the world, back to the early history of humanity, he tends to tell the same story as the speakers of other dialects. Some of the places in his story lie in the geographical territory of his dialect and some are in the territory of other dialects. Thus the Papagos share the same world as far as "mythology" is concerned. They also share a social world, for Papagos marry Papagos and tend to seek each other's company in preference to all other tribes and nationalities.

The fact remains that there is no one authorized version of Papago culture. Each of the more that 20,000 Papagos is a carrier of it although some people

[2]A brief history of the coauthors' work on this project is in order. The project started in 1970 with Bahr's idea to publish the Papago versions of Underhill's texts. Some Papagos, including the three coauthors, had expressed an interest in seeing them, and Underhill felt that publication was desirable. Bahr had by this time taped some of the current versions of the same speeches.

The faculty grant-in-aid program at Arizona State University supported Bahr through the summer of 1972 which he then conceived of as a study of all the available written texts of Pima and Papago oratory, with special emphasis on preparing Underhill's collection for publication. Baptisto and David Lopez freely gave of their time and knowledge for this task. It was not finished, however, and lay dormant until 1975 when Arizona State University gave another grant, this time with stipends for three Papagos—the above two plus Jose Pancho—to complete the job. Bahr at this stage worked on his own time.

The project developed to its present form in which each coauthor made the following contribution: Underhill—read the manuscript at various stages, offered suggestions and corrections, and wrote the section on her work collecting the original texts. Baptisto Lopez—worked with Bahr on texts in 1972, discussed the wine feast speeches with Jose Pancho and Bahr in 1975, taped the narrative of the war campaign. David Lopez—worked with Bahr on texts in 1972 and 1975-8. During this time the two went over most orations more than once to iron out issues of transcription and translation. They specialized in the texts which Jose Pancho did not know. Jose Pancho—read Underhill's versions and taped his own versions of the wine feast and *a'ada* speeches, checked transcription and translation of the same. Bahr—participated with the above as indicated, wrote the commentaries, and has final responsibility for all errors.

The following others are thanked for their contributions and aid in seeing the project through: Adelaide Bahr, Mary Coen, Joseph Giff, Juan Gregorio (c.1900-1971), Jose Moreno (c.1900-1975), Chico Moreno (1923-1976), Victor Moreno, Sylvester Lopez, Sherwood Idso, and Bernard Fontana. Special thanks are also due to Karl Luckert, editor of the series, for his good advice, patience, and encouragement; and to the Museum of Northern Arizona for effecting publication.

certainly are better versed or more interested in the Native traditions than others. The culture thrives through its variations. This is a strength for its survival for it is not dependent on a few individuals. This same trait means that the Papago culture will never be exhaustively studied, for there are too many people to consult.

The same is true of White culture. Whereas Whites commit their most important knowledge to writing, the Papagos commit their most important knowledge to memorized texts of which ritual speeches are one form. Just as no White knows all of his people's books, no Papago knows all of his people's speeches. Just as a book may be read differently by different individuals, a Papago speech may receive different interpretations. If the reader thinks Papago knowledge is easier to exhaust than White knowledge, he is wrong.

As the book proceeds it will become clear that many of our materials come from a few individuals in one village, Santa Rosa. This geographical concentration is an accident of history that started with the arrival of one of the coauthors, Ruth Underhill, onto the reservation in 1931. In her study of Papago

Church at Santa Rosa.
Arizona State Museum, University of Arizona. Photo by Helga Teiwes.

Round House at Santa Rosa.
Arizona State Museum, University of Arizona. Photo by Helga Teiwes.

religion she concentrated on Santa Rosa. The present book is essentially a restudy of the speeches and information on rituals that she collected and published, in English only, in *Papago Indian Religion* (1946). It was therefore natural that the three Papago coauthors of this book, Baptisto Lopez, David Lopez, and Jose Pancho, should be from the same village. They are the best qualified to prepare Underhill's Papago language transcripts of the speeches for publication, to revise the translations where necessary, and to add information on the rituals. Finally the fifth coauthor, Bahr, is also more familiar with Santa Rosa than with any other village. In sum, this book mainly represents one window into the geographical variation of Papago culture. This is not wholly the case, for there will be some materials from other villages (see Map), but there is a clear need for further studies, especially in the west and south of the reservation.

There is another aspect to the subject of Papago religion as a whole, which is where the seven rites of this book fit in the totality of Papago religious practice. We may speak of this totality as involving two historical traditions, Native and Christian, and as also involving two major settings for religious activity, public and private. Papagos know, and most historians would agree with them, when they are engaging in a Native or a Christian rite. Let us not belabor this point. It must be understood, however, that most Papagos are as seriously involved in the one side as in the other. They derive benefits from both traditions and find it possible to believe in both. A full account of Papago religious life must treat both. The present book is limited to the Native sector and does not pretend to be full.

The distinction between public and private pertains in the simplest sense to the places at which the activities of their traditions take place, and in a deeper sense to "whose business it is." Each tradition has its public places. These are the Church and its surroundings for the Christian tradition, and the 'Round House'[3] *(o:las ki:)* and its surroundings for the Native tradition. Both are maintained at community expense for the benefit of everyone who lives in the community. (Both have offices of leadership, however, which are held by individuals and which may be involved in personal and family politics.) The matter of "whose business it is" relates to who is to benefit from or has to know about a given event. If it is community business, the event will be discussed at the public place; if it is personal business, the event will be discussed within the family or between individuals —and the community at large may never hear about it.

TABLE 1

PAPAGO RELIGION AS A WHOLE

	Public:	*Private:*
Native:	Wine feast	Medicine man's diagnosis
	Salt pilgrimage	Ritual cures
	Rabbit hunt	Clay eating
	Deer hunt	Eagle catching
	A'ada	Telling creation story
	War campaign	
	Spring ceremonies	
	Wi:gita	
	"Social dances"	
	Girl's puberty dance	
Christian:	Feasts of the Christian year	Prayer vigils
	Christian sacraments	Prayers before meals
	Pilgrimages to Christian shrines	All Souls' Day
		Private celebrations of feast days

[3] Single quotes indicate literal translations of Papago words.

Table 1 classifies the whole religious culture in regard to the two dimensions. The rites studied in this book are the first seven of the native and public sector. Once the whole is compartmentalized as in Table 1, one naturally asks how the sectors communicate, as to whether there are religious events—rites and their liturgies—which cross boundaries. A serious attempt to answer that question is beyond the scope of this book, although we will deal with aspects of it in passing. The book will serve a good purpose if it provides materials for such an attempt at a later time. Let us now simply note where interested persons may find materials on the other sectors.

Underhill's *Papago Indian Religion* (1946) covers the whole. Richard Jones (1971: 1-29) has written a summary article on what is known of the very important *wi:gita* ritual (excluded from this book because we lack speeches from it). Richard Haefer has written on the varieties of Papago music and dance, including the "social dances" (1977). Bahr, Gregorio, Lopez, and Alvarez treated the private and native system of curing (1973). Saxton and Saxton (1973), Wright (1929), and Bahr (1970) have written on the creation story. Joseph, Spicer, and Chesky (1949) and Griffith (1975:21-36) have written on Christian fiestas.

SPEECH AND ACT

The words used in any ritual must somehow declare the meaning of the acts. They typically do this in two directions: towards gods or spirits, and towards the participants themselves. Sometimes the liturgy is divided so that some speeches are directed primarily towards one audience (as in prayers) and others towards the other (as in sermons). Where do the speeches of this book stand? We call them "ritual orations." The Papago term for them is *niokculida* 'to talk for somebody's benefit'.

Ritual orations are considered to be words of the ancients. The orator simply repeats them. These orations begin with short passages addressed to the present audience, they then commence to tell the story of an ancient person's travels, supposedly in that person's own words. They end with another short statement addressed to the present human audience. They are like "scripture" in a Christian service. The "somebody" to whom they are addressed is both the present human audience and a divine power who watches over the proceedings.

Some orations are understood to be the words of a well known person of long ago—of a person whose life and deeds are known from the creation story. Most of them are not of that sort, but are the words of ancient persons whose names are no longer known.

These words of the ancients may or may not near a clear surface relationship with the concrete acts performed in a given ritual. Sometimes the relation is close, as, for example, when in the war campaign enemy killers are doused with cold water while an oration is given about the washing of an ancient individual. Often the relation seems more remote, as when a man goes to another village to invite the people from there to a wine feast. The speech that he gives sounds as if he has traveled to the end of the earth to obtain clouds. There is an important abstract relation between speech and rite, however, which is that each oration is based on the idea of a single hero's journey to a distant place and back; and each rite requires a journey to a distant place and back.

To be more specific, each rite will be discussed as having five *phases*.

1. Preparations for departure.
2. The Journey out.
3. Arriving at a place to get something.
4. The Journey back.
5. Celebration of the return.

As we follow the sequence through the rites, two things will be seen. First, the entire process may take various amounts of time, from as little as the daylight portion of one day to an entire month; and second, a given phase may or may not be ceremonialized in a given rite. Thus, the preparation phase sometimes is initiated with an oration, and sometimes it is not. A third observation is also in order, namely, that oratory is not the only form of speech used in Papago ceremonies. Song is another very important form, certainly as important as oratory in giving the meaning of the rites. There are also many speeches resembling sermons, that is, speeches addressed to the participants of a rite giving them instructions or telling them directly how they should think or feel. Oratory does this indirectly with its stories of the ancients. Finally, people may simply talk with each other. We do not exclude these other forms of speech from the present book because they are unimportant. Their study is for the future.

Turning now to the plan of the typical oration, such a speech has the following components:

1. A *preface* states what the hero did before commencing his journey.
2. A *body* contains several *parts*, each describing a portion of his journey. The typical *part* has the form: the hero sets out, he travels, he arrives someplace, and he does something.
3. A *conclusion* states what happened as the result of his journey.

It is understood, of course, that orations usually are given at several points during a rite. Thus we must consider how the progression of speeches corresponds with the progression of the rite; usually it is not a question of studying a single speech, but of studying a set of them.

This book is not meant as a technical treatise on oratory. It consists largely of English translations and little linguistic analysis will be offered. It is based on a distinct theory of oratorical composition, but we will not overemphasize that theory. As informally as possible, we will point out how individual speeches conform to or depart from it. The interested reader is referred to a book by Bahr which gives a detailed analysis of three versions of a single speech (1975). The orations given here are written in conformity with the ideas of that book. A total of twenty-four different texts are given, representing seven different orators and five different villages.

TRANSCRIPTION AND TRANSLATION

Readers who are not interested in writing and translating Indian texts may skip this section. The following problems are discussed: establishing the proper version of a text, orthography, and translation. The context in which we deal with them is as follows—each text in the book was originally transcribed and translated by Underhill in the 1930s. The question is, "What can another White and three Papagos add to her contribution?"

Concerning the proper version of a text, we understand that orations are targeted for word for word accuracy from one recitation to the next. This is not the most stringent goal Papagos set for themselves in their oral literature. Songs are meant to be sung with sound for sound accuracy; they are memorized "letter perfect." One does not know a song until he has it down to the last twitch of the tongue.

Word for word accuracy means that certain sounds may be left off the ends of words in one recitation and be put on again in the next, and that "unimportant" words and quasi words—auxiliaries—may be contracted, expanded, or omitted. Also, complete accuracy may not be attained. Whole words may be changed and, in rare instances, lines may be exchanged or deleted from one recitation to another. It must be understood that these are long texts, from five to ten minutes in length. The flux and variation between recitations is real, but one's overall impression is of extreme control.

The implication of this for writing the "proper" text is that we write with letters representing individual sounds, but in reality there is a certain amount of flux. We are often faced with the choice of either writing a line "just as he said it" or of writing it in a longer or otherwise corrected form as it might have been said if the speaker were not in a hurry, or if he had not made a "mistake."

When Underhill and her principal Papago assistant, Juan Havier, wrote their original texts in the 1930s, they lacked a consistent set of rules for making those choices. While we have found points to correct in their transcriptions, we also lack rules. The corrections are arbitrary. A concise way to state the problem is to say that neither Bahr nor Underhill offer a theory of oratorical "diction." It is known that oratory is a special way of speaking, roughly midway between ordinary speech and song—"chant" in other words. Many of the problems concerning long and short ways of saying or writing a line might be resolved if the diction of oratory were approached as a system of rules unto itself. This has not been achieved.

A final point must be made on this matter. It was possible to record later versions of many of the speeches which Underhill collected in the 1930s. These are either from the same orator or from a successor. In this book we have always used those later speeches because they were "backed" by a tape recording which could be consulted for making revisions in transcription.

The second issue is orthography. The texts are written in an orthography developed by Albert Alvarez and Kenneth Hale (1970). When she collected the texts, Underhill used an orthography which did not show the difference between what Hale and Alvarez identify as 'sharp' and 'mellow' consonants. As this difference is significant in Papago, the Hale and Alvarez orthography is an improvement. Various other orthographies also make this distinction, but the one we use has the formal support of the Papago Tribe.

An orthography is only as good as the ear of its user, that is, one should understand the linguistic analysis on which it is based and one must hear the relevant distinctions in a spoken text. We have probably misheard and misspelled a good number of words. In many instances we have been arbitrary in deciding what should stand by itself as a word, a problem with relates to the above discussion on diction.

The final topic is translation. Orations are by nature difficult to understand. They do not give their meanings away, but demand interpretation. Making a translation requires an interpretation in a sense that simply repeating a speech in one's own language does not. One can learn a speech by simply getting its sounds —by memorizing it (as mocking bird does in one of the speeches given below). One has gotten the sounds, but what about the meaning?

Translation is a very simple test of whether one has grasped the meaning of something. Translation requires an interpretation in which the sounds of the original are of no help. Once one has decided what a passage means in a second language, he may then try to express that meaning in a manner that sounds like the original. But the act of interpretation comes first.

Translation is difficult work. It is also perpetually unfinished work. There is no last, perfect translation. The English translations in this book represent an early stage in the art of interpreting Papago oratory. They are not the first but the second stage. The first stage was accomplished by Underhill and Havier. The translations presented here differ from those of the first stage in virtually every line of text. The differences are not great, but they do exist.

Our translations are based on Underhill's field notebooks which are much more literal (word for word) than the translations which she published in *Papago Indian Religion*. We have kept the translations as literal as possible, that is, closer to the level of Underhill's field notebooks than to her "freer" published versions. This has resulted in some changes, especially in word order. Furthermore, we have tried to use the vocabulary of everyday English rather than literary or Biblical language, for example to write "Look" rather than "Lo," or "brave" rather than "doughty."

We have frequently differed from Underhill and Havier in interpreting the specific sense of a line. For example, the following is the transcription, the literal (notebook) translation, and the free (published) translation of one line by Underhill and Havier:

> Wacak hi a:kit hi w'i'nat hi hap t-tcun.
> There go tell go together went thus doing.
> Come, admit it! I will treat you as I would them.

Here is how we now transcribe and translate the same line:

> Wa:ṣ heg i a:gk heg we:nad i hab t-ju:nan.
> Yes, go ahead and tell it and together we can die.

This example shows the different orthographies, differences in word divisions, and how this book's level of translation falls between Underhill's literal and free levels. In short it shows everything that was discussed above. Let us now note how the new translation differs in meaning from the old: (a) There are different shades of meaning between "tell" and "admit;" (b) The presence of an "I" in one translation and a "we" in the other represents quite different readings. The 'we' is literally correct, the 'I' is literally in error; (c) Underhill and Havier saw this statement as being made by the hero of the text to an 'enemy'; we see it the other way around; (d) The interpretations of the final phrase differ as to whether death is at issue.

What we have shown here is but one line out of thousands. It was picked because the differences in it are substantial (it is from the 'Cure Speech' of the war campaign), but it is far from unique. We feel that the new version is correct, but that correctness is a matter of degree. The old translation was not "And quiet flowed the Don" or some other completely absurd reading of the Papago original. Our interpretation could have missed something, too. Yet, we have not hesitated to differ from the earlier translations. It is felt that two available translations, consistently made, are better than one. The interested reader may want to study the earlier translations side by side with the present ones. We have not footnoted the differences because they are so many.

Where we have not wished to differ with the originals is when we did not know a word or were otherwise completely baffled by a passage. This did not often happen. When it did it was mostly in dealing with texts from villages other than Santa Rosa and with rites that the Papago coauthors were unfamiliar with.

A major guide in our translation is the theory of oratorical composition sketched in the previous section. The theory obliges one to look for a context in which the same hero is in action throughout a text, and to look for language concerned with journeying. These factors have influenced our word choices as well as our construals of plot. Without that theory, the present retranslation project would not have been attempted, for we would have had nothing new to add to Underhill's and Havier's earlier contribution. The best way to define the present "stage two," then, is to view it as "the journey theory stage."

A final point on the application of that theory should be mentioned. In its original form it specified what should be written as a line of text and how texts should be punctuated (1975:21-22). We have not followed those specifications consistently with the present texts for a reason stated in the original work. There are other factors to consider in defining lines and sentences, such as pauses, intonation, etc. Eventually a theory of oratorical diction will be called for, perhaps as a future "stage three."

Saguaro cactus
in bloom.
Photo by
Karl W. Luckert

Rain

THE PAPAGO YEAR

Here we consider when the year starts and how it is reckoned. Let us begin with a negative point: The start of the year has nothing directly to do with the sun. The important times of the solar year, as Papagos and probably all cultures know, are the two solstices (the longest and the shortest days of the year, June 21 and December 21 in the European calendar) and the two equinoxes (March 21 and September 21, when days and nights are of equal length).

Some Papagos call the 'month' (*maṣad*, 'moon', 'month') of the winter solstice the 'Backbone month' *(eḍa wa'ugad maṣad)* because the solstice seems to divide the year in halves. This is the one reference to the sun in the system of month names. The 'Backbone month' was the favored time to tell the creation story, the most favored time of all being the four longest nights of the year which bracket the solstice. This is the only ritual that was prescribed for that time. It is a native and private ritual according to the classification of Table 1; it is not one of the public rites which are the subject matter of this book.

If the ritual cycle that we are interested in has nothing directly to do with the sun, what does it have to do with? The answer is, "the clouds of summer." The first rite to be discussed, the summer wine feast, is actually a New Year's celebration. The rite begins, without oratory, with the picking of saguaro cactus fruits. Depending on the year and the place, these are ready for picking from late June to late July—they miss the solstice. The fruits are picked, some are dried, some are boiled into jam, and some are boiled into syrup. On returning to the village, the syrup is made into wine for the wine feast. This feast, with its initial nights of singing and dancing, its 'sit and drink' *(dahiwak i:)* with oratory, and its final days and nights of celebration, is the most notable part of the ritual. It all belongs to phase 5 according to the scheme presented in the Introduction.

Wine feasts are held at different times in different villages, and not all villages have them. Underhill found them to be a feature of the northern rather than the southern Papagos, a point that we will return to in a later chapter concerned with hunting rites. The point for now is that where they exist, they celebrate the rain clouds which begin to arrive in Papago country from the east at about the same time as the cactuses ripen. The relation of the three "seasons"—cactus picking, rain storms, and wine feasts—is as given in Table 2. It is seen that the rainy season begins ahead of the wine feasts and tails off with them.

TABLE 2

CACTUS, RAIN, AND WINE FEAST SEASONS

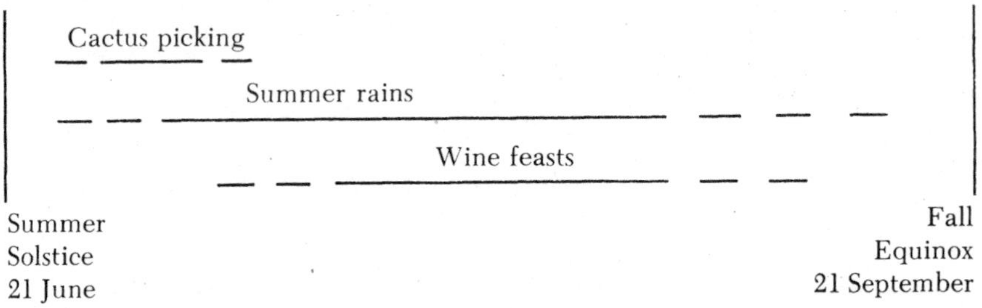

We continue this discussion of time reckoning with Table 3 which presents the month names (or 'moons') collected by Russell from the Pima (1908:36), and Saxton and Saxton (1969:78-81) and Underhill (1939:124-25) from the Papago. It is seen that 'Saguaro ripe month' precedes 'Rainy month' in three of the lists; the two names are alternatives in one list. Some additional comments are in order. These are names of *moons*, that is, of lunar cycles. As such they are unlike the months of the European calendar which always begin on the same day of the solar year. A lunar cycle is about 29 and one half days long; there are about 12 and two fifths lunar cycles in the 365 and one fourth day solar year. In short, nothing fits very well. It may be noted that three of the lists give 12 months, one gives 13.

The Papago months are really short seasons, that is, Papagos know a progression of seasons (rain, cactus picking, etc.) and these seasons are used to name moons. Looking at the meanings of the names in Table 3, we may conclude that the year is divided into three large segments of four 'moons' each. The first segment concerns rain and farming—from 'Saguaro ripe moon' to 'Dry grass moon' (meaning that the rains are over and the earth is dry again). The second concerns the cold—from 'Surviving moon' (meaning that the frosts have come and not all plants can survive—Saxton and Saxton, 1969:179) to 'Lean moon' (meaning that deer and rabbits are lean and not fat). The last group of moon names concerns the growth of new vegetation in spring, both of grasses and wild flowers whose appearance depends on winter rains ('Yellow moon'), and of trees whose flowers and leaves come out whether it has rained that month or not. Finally, the last month name is the anticipation of the first one: 'Black seeds' refers to the seeds of saguaro cactus which turn black when the fruits are almost ready to pick.

A final point on time reckoning: It is doubtful whether the Papagos had a system of weeks and weekdays before the Spanish came. If they did, there is no sign of it now, for the names of the days are in Spanish. If they had it and lost it, one wonders why they lost that and not their system of lunar months. In any case, as we discuss the rites of the ritual year in the following chapters it will be seen that the concept of the *week*, certainly the seven day week, is missing. Dates are set according to when the (lunar) season is right. Periods of two, four, ten, and sixteen days are significant in various rituals, but there is no mention of a seven day period.

As so much of today's life is regulated by the European system of five "working days" and two-day "weekends," it is difficult to imagine a life without this system. It is suggested that the old timers had such a life and, it may be added, the importance of working days and weekends in the present economy is one of the reasons why the old ritual cycle has proved difficult to uphold. Virtually all of the ceremonies in this book require more than two days and two nights to carry out, so they do not lend themselves to the free time on weekends left by the European system.

TABLE 3

MOON NAMES

Russell:	*Russell:*	*Saxton and Saxton:*	*Underhill:*
	Wheat harvest		
Saguaro ripe	Saguaro ripe	Saguaro ripe	Rainy, Saguaro ripe
Rainy	Rainy	Rainy	
Short planting	Short planting	Short planting	Short planting, Big rain
Dry grass	Dry grass	Dry grass	Dry grass
Cold	Windy	Surviving	Small rain, Frost
Yellow	Smelly	Fair cold	Pleasant cold
Leaves falling	Big winter	Backbone	Big cold
Cottonwood flowers	Gray	Lean	Thin
Cottonwood leaves	Green	Odor	Smelling, Gray
Mesquite leaves	Yellow	Gray	Green
Mesquite flowers	Strong	Green	Yellow
Black seeds		Yellow	Mesquite buds, Painful
		Painful, Grain cutting	Seeds black

THE WINE FEAST

As was stated above, the public ritual of the Papago New Year is confined to the rite's final phase, the celebration on returning home from a journey. The journey is to cactus camps to pick fruit and make syrup. Let us start from the beginning and trace the whole process.

Most families maintain separate territories for picking cactus. These territories are not fixed like ranches or fields—they are not fenced—but they are meant to be respected. In the midst of a family's territory is a simple camp; an open walled sunshade (*ramada* in Spanish, *watto* in Papago), a fireplace, and little more. These, however, are somebody's place just as surely as a house is.

Prior to the cactus picking season Papago families tended to be dispersed, especially in former times. This was the 'Painful moon' when food was scarce.

Saguaro cactus laden with fruit. Heard Museum. Photo by Jon Erickson.

Left: Cactus picking. Arizona State Museum, University of Arizona. Photo by Helga Teiwes.

One family might have gone to live near a well in the mountains. Another might go to Mexico to work in the wheat harvest which comes in May or June. Others might go to the Pimas for the same reason. (One of the Pima calendars in Table 3 starts with the wheat harvest rather than the ripening of saguaro fruits.) Wherever a family was, and it might vary from year to year, going to the cactus camp would require a move. The preparations for this move usually were not ceremonialized.[1]

When a family arrives at its camp there is one bit of private ritual. Each person is supposed to take the first ripe fruit that he encounters, open it, extract some of its juicy, red pulp, apply it to his heart, and say a prayer of thanks for having lived another year. Then there would be one, two, or three weeks of picking, eating, cooking, drying, and storing fruits. If there were extra men, some might hunt. These were usually happy weeks as there were usually far more fruits than could be consumed. They were weeks of plenty.

The one complication in this period is rain which, if it comes, can wash away the ripe and opened fruit and set the picking back two or three days until a new batch has opened. (Each cactus can produce 50 to 100 fruits which open at different times during the three week period.) It is important to note, then, that the wine feast is not to start the rain, but to keep it raining, for it usually rains during the picking season. It is also important to note this remarkable thing about saguaro fruits, that they reach moist, ripe maturity without rain. Some even say that they do not like rain, that is, if it rains much in the spring, they will not produce much fruit.

The journey home is no more ceremonialized than the preparations or the journey out. Upon arrival, which in old times might be the first time a village had recongregated since the preceding winter, the next step is to set the date for the

[1]Only sometimes they were, as in Mesquite Root, as discussed in the chapter on Flood.

wine feast (*nawait i'ita*, literally, 'wine drinks'). This is done at a meeting at night in the village 'round house' *(o:las ki:)*.

This building figures prominently in the planning and celebration stages of every rite. It is of the type of house that people used to live in, although nobody lives in the village round house. It is a public building, not anyone's private structure. Immediately to the east of the round house is a sunshade *(watto)*. To the east of that is a large area of cleared ground with a place in the middle for making a fire. These three places—round house, *watto*, and ceremonial ground—are all significant in the account of the wine feast that follows.

The rite has been described at length by Underhill in *Papago Indian Religion* (1946:41-67) and in other of her writings (especially 1936 and 1939). Here we will only outline it with special emphasis on the speeches.

The date is set, syrup is collected from each family for brewing in the round house, and each family also sets a separate household supply to brewing. The

Cactus camp. Heard Museum. Photo by Jon Erickson.

Earliest known picture of Papagos, a lithograph of a pithaya harvest by Arthur Schott, made for the *United States and Mexican Boundary Survey,* 1857.

brewing process may take as few as two days (as Underhill was told and the speeches say), or a longer time may be allowed for it. In any case the public ceremonial activity at the round house begins two nights before the village supply will be ready.

Each of those nights is spent in singing and dancing on the cleared ground around a fire to the east of the *watto*. The songs are called *gohimeli* songs, named for the "scissors" step of the dancers. Men and women join hands to dance counterclockwise around the fire in a large circle. Inside the dancers' circle, near the fire, a medicine man (or more) works through the nights to find out when and how it will rain in the future. This combination of a medicine man working in the night while people sing, occurs in nearly every ceremony described in this book. To the west of the dancing ground, under the *watto*, sit one or more old people who start and stop each song that is sung. Sixteen songs are typically sung through the night in four groups of four, but the number and pacing may vary at the discretion of the old singers who are in charge. Between the groups of songs are rest periods when, as Underhill was told, romances might develop or at least be contemplated. It is not a time of license, however.

Between the first and second nights of singing was an optional rabbit hunt which we discuss in the chapter on hunting. The next fixed event in the ceremony is at dawn after the second night. Then the first sample of wine is brought out. Not much is drunk at this time. Single baskets of wine are given to the medicine man and to the leading singers and dancers. They serve it to whomever gathers around them. Soon it is over and nearly everyone goes home to rest for the next important event of the day, the 'sit and drink' *(dahiwak i:)*, around noon.

One or more men have another task to do. They are to 'run' (now ride) to three neighboring villages to invite the people there to the sit and drink. These men speak the first ritual oration of the wine feast, called the 'running speech' *(melida ñiok)*. It is delivered to a man sitting before the round house of the invited village. This and the other wine feast speeches given below are from Santa Rosa. Underhill recorded them from Jose Moreno. The versions given below are from Jose Pancho. Since Underhill's time, one or another of the speeches has also been delivered by Chico Moreno, Victor Moreno, and perhaps others. Each orator has a very slightly different version of the speeches. Thus, the versions given here are slightly different from the texts taken down by Underhill. Only a specialist would know the difference, however, and it cannot be said that the speeches have gotten shorter or lost any important content between 1930 and 1978.

The man of the invited village to whom the speech is addressed responds with a "mate" to it called the 'return running' *(melida ab wui ce:)*. Both speeches start by describing the poor conditions of the land before it rains. The inviter says in the preface that his homeland is dry and pitiful. The invited man responds by describing a similar scene in slightly different words, but in reference to the inviter's homeland. This is the pattern of the pair of speeches: The 'return' speech tells essentially the same story as the first one, only it tells it from the respondent's point of view substituting all of the "I's" of the first speech with "you's" and *vice versa*.

As the story proceeds, it becomes progressively unlike anything that the actual speakers could literally have done. In place of the 'round house' at the invited village, the speeches refer to a 'rainhouse' (*wa'aki*—the word doesn't literally mean 'rain' plus 'house'; this is only our translation of the sense of this word) that the inviter reached by traveling a shining road. The house is full of winds, clouds, and seeds. In short, the man being invited is addressed as a god. When his turn comes to speak, he responds in kind, repeating the essentials of the story that the 'runner' has told to him.

RUNNING SPEECH

Jose Pancho, Santa Rosa

Na'an s-melidameḍ, idañ am a ep mel, e:p.	Am I not the runner, now I've run here again.
Hascu am a ge s-keg ñ-taccuidag c id hab e-ju:.	Something good is my desire and now it is happened.
Kuñ wa pi ñ-ma:c.	At first I didn't know.
Has ma:s u:s ṣon ab kupal ka:c	At some kind of tree bottom face down [I] lay
Ta haskojeḍ hewel i meḍ, g jeweḍ i wi'um	From someplace a wind ran, dirt it stirred up
K ab ñ-wuhyo ha'as wua	And messed my face
Tanhadag wakomegidag i wi'umk ñ-mo'o si ṣa:ṣa'ig.	Trash and garbage it stirred up and plastered in my hair.
I	I
Nt a i wu:ṣ	Then I emerged
Ñ-hugid an da:kam ñ-hajuñ ab si ha-i:mk ṣoṣa	To my nearby sitting relatives I kinship cried
Kut a am ge s-ñ-ho'ige'idam e-ta:t k he'es ha'u go'ol wasipk ñ-ma:.	Towards me they very kindly felt, a little dipper's remains [of syrup] to me they gave.
Kuñ g ṣu:dagi ab iolagidk he'es ha'a go'ol tua	Then I the water mixed with it and a little pot's remains [of wine makings] I put
Cem si s-oiyucud taccu	Hoping for speed [in winemaking]
Kuñ g wui am mu:giakc am daha.	Towards it I bent over and sat.
II	II
Kuñ a wa ñ-ki: a:gc wu:sañk	I thought of my house and emerged
Am cem him, baṣo i noḍagk am u:pam wua	Just went, in front of it turned and returned back again
Ta am si ñ-ho'ige'idk go:k si'alig ge s-keg e-ai.	Then it [wine] pitied me and two days later beautifully was ready.
Hebai da:kam ñ-wepo taccuikam am hahawa i cegito	The someplace sitting people that desire like me I then remembered
Ta i m-wui wo:g si tonoḍk e-ce:k.	The road towards you shined brightly and was put.

III

Ant a heba'i ṣoṣ
Ko wa wuḍ ñ-hewelig, am ñ-ai
Am a ge s-wa'usim meḍ
Kuñ heg ta : tkc hab cu'ijig.

III

I made a stop
There was my wind and it reached me
There very wetly it ran
I felt it and did things.

IV

Nt a hebai ep ṣoṣ
Ko wa wuḍ g ñ-cewagig, am ñ-ai
Am ge s-wa'usim si : bañ
Ta i : ya si ce : mo'o g m-wa'akik cem ñei.

Ha'akia hewel ab ka : c, ha'aki cewagi ab ka : c, ha'akia ha'icu kaikam ab ka : c
Pt ag da'iṣc ab daha
Tag we : nadk ab si m-ta : t.
Kutp a i hoink i i : bheiwa e-hewelig

Tag we : nadk i hab i i-juccuhimk
Ia dagitoñ ñ-jeweḍga da : m
Heg hekaj g ñ-jeweḍga am ge s-keg wa'opagidk na : ato.

Tag da : m ab wu : ṣ

Hejel wu : ṣkam e-a : g
T am ge s-keg e-bai
Heg hekaj am hahawa ge s-kekegam huḍuñig, ge s-kekegam ma : sidag.
Kut oi hebai hab a cem ma : skad
K ag hebai has am t-cu'ijig.

Kupt oi am has i i-juñhimk himk ab ba : g ṣu : dagi ñ-na : to.

IV

I made another stop
There was my cloud and it reached me
There very wetly it sprinkled
Now here I reached your rainhouse and looked.

Many winds here lay, many clouds here lay, many seeds here lay
And you set them down and sat on them
[I] Joined with them and touched you.
And so you moved and breathed your wind

With it [you were] doing things
Here [you] dropped it on my land
From that my land is wet and finished.

On top of that [land] something came out

It thought it came out by itself
Then got nice and ripe
From that there were good evenings, good mornings [for us].
This sometime will come true
And when it does it will be from what we did.

So you may come along and drink the water [wine] I have made.

RETURN TO THE RUNNING

Jose Pancho, Santa Rosa

Heu'u, bat ki hems e-ju : g hebai ha'icu'i m-taccuidag
Map e-jeweḍga e-a : g
Map ag da : m an a'i cem ke : kiup, apt a cem ñeid.
Gamai si ṣo'ig ma : sc ka : c
Do : da'ag cu : cim si mo : mgi'ak e-cu : cia

U'us pi hahakc cu : c

Yes, perhaps it happened what you wished for
What you intended for your land
On top of which you stood and looked.

It looked pitiful as it lay
Mountains were standing but were rotten as they stood

Trees were without leaves as they stood

Kupt ag am cem ñeidk
Am hab ju: g hab cu'igam ha'icu
e-taccuidag.

That is what you saw and
Then it happened what you wished for.

I

In haha wa we:gaj i ne:nhog
Kan i ñei g we:gaj da:kam e-hajuñ
Hab hahawa si ha-i:mk ṣosa̤.
Ta ab he'es ha'u go'ol m-wasib

Ta he'es ha'a go'ol tua
Kup g wui am mu:giak
Cem si s-oiyucudc.

I

Then around yourself you looked
And saw your nearby sitting relatives
Then to them kinship cried.
A little dipper's remains [of syrup] they
poured for you
A little pot's remains [you] put
Towards it you bent over and sat
Hoping for speed.

II

At ki am ge s-m-ho'ige'idam e-ta:t
K am go:k si'al am ge s-keg e-ai
Kupt a hebai g e-wepo taccuikam haha
wa i cegito
Kut a ñ-wui wo:g si tonodk e-ce:k

K ia ñ-ai.

II

Kindly to you it felt
And two days later beautifully it finished.
The someplace sitting people that desire
like you you then remembered
The road to me shined bright and
was put
Reaching me here.

III

Kupt ag oidc hab cu'ijig
Idañ ia si ñ-ce:mo'o
Cem ñei g ñ-wa'aki mab ke:k.

Eḍa ha'akia hewel ab ka:c, ha'akia
cewagi ab ka:c, ha'akia ha'icu kai
ab ka:c
Kuñ ag daiṣc im daha
Kupt ag we:nadk ab si ñ-ta:t.

Kunt ha'ap i hoi
Ab i i:bhei g ñ-hewelig, ab i himc
g ñ-cewagig
Kunt ag we:nad i hab i ñ-juccuhim
Kunt a am dagitoñ m-jeweḍga da:m
Heg hekaj g m-jeweḍga am ge s-keg
e-wa'akpan ce:k e-na:to.

At ag da:m am wu:ṣ g ha'icu kai

A hejel wu:skam e-a:g
At a am ge s-keg bai.
Heg o a wesko da:kam t-hajuñ wuḍ
wuikam c hab e-ju:

III

So you followed it and did things
Now here you reached me
You look at my rainhouse that here
stands.

In it many winds here lay, many clouds
here lay, many seeds here lay

And I set them down and sat on them
You joined with them and touched me.

And so I moved
[I] Breathed my wind, my cloud started

With it I was doing things
And these [doings] I drop on your land
From that your land is wetly put and
finished.

On top of that [land] came out a seeded
thing
It thought it came out by itself
Then got nice and ripe.
Yet all our relatives are the reason for it
and that's why it happened

Kut ag hekaj am haha wa ge s-kegkam huḍuñig, s-kegkam ma:sidag.	From that there were good evenings, good mornings.
Ñe:, ha'ap hems a'i elidk o taccu ñ-nawoj	Look, this you may wish and plan, my friend
Oi an hebai hab cem ma:skad g ha'icu t-cu'ijig	Then sometime surely something will come true from what we did
Nt oi an has iñ-juñhimk	So I will now start it off
Oi am o him, k am o i: g ṣu:dagi m-jewajida.	And will go, will drink the water you have rotted.

Following the exchange of speeches the 'runner' returns home. The invited villagers arrive some hours later, usually around noon, at the outskirts of the ceremonial ground of the village. They wait there until another speech is delivered to them, called the 'seating speech' *(dadṣpa ñiok)*. The speaker is the same man who gave the 'running' speech earlier in the day. After this speech the visiting party is escorted, running again, to its assigned place at the ceremonial ground—east, south, or north. The host village occupies the west. Once all the parties are seated, the 'sit and drink' is ready to begin.

SEATING SPEECH

Jose Pancho, Santa Rosa

Kuñ a wa hab a'i cu'ijig g ñ-nawoj, idañ am a ep mel, e:p.	So I did it my friend, now I have run up here again.
An o hebai ha'icu am wuḍ ge s-kehegam ñ-taccuidag c id hab e-ju:.	Somewhere something good is my desire and now it has happened.
Kuñ wa pi ñ-ma:c.	At first I didn't know.
I	I
An cem ba:ñmeḍk pi ñ-na:ko	I crawled off and couldn't stand it
Ko ki wa ñ-uwiwa, ñ-alowa hejel ha'icu an s-ma:c	But there was my girl, my boy, who something seemed to know
At a'i bebbehim, iñ-matk eḍ si daṣwa.	They brought it here, in my hand they placed it [syrup].
Kunt ag ṣu:dagi am si iolig	Then I the water mixed with it
He'es ha'a go'ol toa	A little pot of remains [of winemaking] I put.
An a heg wui am mu:gia'akc am daha	Towards it I bent over then and sat
Am cem si s-oiyucudc taccu.	Hoping for speed.
II	II
Kuñ wa ñ-ki: a:gc am wu:ṣañ	I thought of my house and came out
Am cem himk baṣo iñ-himnogidk am upam wua	Just went in front of it, turned and returned back again
Hejelp ñ-we:m ñiok, t ab dagihuñ	Talked to myself and wiped it [pot of wine]

Ta am s-ñ-ho'ige'id e-ta : tk am go : k
si'alim ge s-keg e-ai.
Kunt a hebai da : kam ma : kai haha
i cegito
Kunt m-wui wo : g si tonoḍk e-ce : k

Ia m-ai
Kuñ oidk hab cu'ijig.

Then it pitied me and in two days was
beautifully finished.
The someplace sitting medicine man I
then remembered
The road towards you shined bright and
was put
Reaching you here
And I followed and did things.

III

Kunt a hebai ṣoṣ
Ko ki a wa wuḍ a ñ-hewelig
Am ñ-ai.
Ge s-ap ta : hadam s-wa'osim meḍ
Kuñ ag ta : t c hab cu'ijig.

III

And I made a stop
There was my wind
And it reached me.
So very nice and wetly it ran
I felt it and did things.

IV

Kunt a hebai ep ṣoṣ
Ki kia wa wuḍ a ñ-cewagig
Am ñ-ai.
Ge s-ap ta : hadam s-wa'osim si : bañ
Kuñ g ta : t c hab cu'ijig.
Ant a'i si m-ce : mo'o, cem ñei
C eḍa hekihu si m-ki : kio ṣoṣon si
wapawañ cu : c, m-cecenodag ṣoṣon si
wapawañ cu : c

Am we : cim ṣu : dagi ha'as ṣo'oṣpol i wo : p
Weco s-mamatodagc ka : c
Kunt ag am si s-ho : hoidk am si
kawoḍkadk bei.

IV

I made another stop
There was my cloud
It reached me.
Very nice and wetly it sprinkled
I felt it and did things.
I reached you and looked
Inside [your rainhouse] your wall
straighteners bases already wetly
stood, your house posts' bases very
wetly stood
Around it water shortly ran
Below it water plants lay
I liked it and gathered it up.

V

Ant a'i wu : ṣañk an m-we : gaj i ne : nhog
O kia wa wuḍ a ñ-to : da'aga, hekihu an
ge hikṣpi kikihodagc cu : c

Weco g jeweḍ s-mamatodagc ka : c

Ant am si s-ho : hoidk am si kawoḍkadk
bei.

V

I emerged and around you [I] looked
It was my mountains, already with
drizzles arched over them [they]
stood
Below them the earth covered with
waterplants lay
I liked it and gathered it up.

VI

Ant a'i upam ha'ahog i ñ-wua
Kunt am i ep oid t-wo : ga mim ka : c
An ce : mo'o g ñ-wa'aki mab ke : k

VI

Then homeward I turned
Followed our road that lay there
Reached my rainhouse that there stands

Ko kia eḍa ha'akia hewel ab ka:c,
ha'akia cewagi ab ka:c, ha'akia
ha'icu kai ab ka:c.
Kuñ eḍa hekihu im hab i juñcugc ant
ha'ap si we:nad
Ta hekaj g ñ-do:da'aga hekihu ge hikṣp
kikihodagc cu:c.
Kunt a eḍa hekiu am ge s-wepegim wasib
tua
Kuñ ag i'ihik m-a:gc wui am i
m-wanckwa
K g wui am m-daṣwa.
Kupt a ab ba:, kupt a ab i:k
Ge s-keg nawam, s-keg noḍa
Am apt haha pi ñ-huwit ge s-keg ha'icu
a:ga
S-keg e-ce:cki, s-keg e-ñe'ñei.
Kupt ag wi'idag i bebbehin
K e-wo'ikuḍ ce:mo'o
K g weco am hiaṣ
Apt ag wi'idaj ia dagitoñ
T ag n-wo'ikuḍ ce:mo'o
K g weco am hiaṣ
K g ep hi wo'iṣ k ia wo'iwa.

Ta am go:k si'alim
At a si'alig tagiojeḍ g hewel si s-e-ma:c
k i meḍ
Tag oidk i hi:, ge s-wa'ag ka:cim.

Ko wa wuḍ ge na:nko t-cu'ickud
Kutt a am si s-keg wapan ce:k na:to.
Ñe:, ha'ap t hems a'i elid k taccu
ñ-nawoj
Oi a has am i i-ju: k o him, ba'an
g ṣu:dagi ñ-jewajda.

And in it many winds lay, many clouds
lay, many seeds lay.

In it I had already done something and
that way I joined it
From that my mountains already with
drizzles arched over them stood.
In there [rainhouse] already the red
serving I had put
I told you to drink it and towards it
pulled you
Towards it sat you.
You swallowed it, you drank it
Beautifully drunk, beautifully dizzy
You didn't keep from me the good talk

Your good dreams, good songs.
And the leftovers you took
To your bed [you] arrived
Below it [you] buried them [leftovers].
But some leftovers you dropped off here
To my bed [I] arrived
Below it [I] buried them
Lay them down and lay on it.

Then two mornings [passed]
Then the wind from the east understood
and ran
Continued and went, [so there was]
wetness lying.
And that was what we did
How we wetly put it [earth] and finished.
Look, thus you may wish and plan
my friend
Come now and do something and go,
drink the water that I have rotted.

This speech is similar to the first two in starting with a man in desolation. He is given some wine makings. Once they have finished brewing, in two days, he sets off for the inhabitant of a distant rainhouse. As in the 'running' speech he is followed by his own wet wind, a detail of the narrated story which signals a departure from what could be literally true of the Papago giving the speech. Arriving at the other's rainhouse, he finds a fabulous wetness and helps himself to what he wants—water plants. In this speech there is no physical contact with the owner of the house. (In the 'running' speech he 'touches' the owner and the owner responds by breathing clouds to wet the inviter's land.)

The 'seating speech'. Drawing by Mike Chiago.

The 'seating' speech then continues with some episodes not found in the previous speeches. The hero returns back to his own 'rainhouse' where winds, clouds, and seeds lay just as they were found in the 'rainhouse' of the other. In short, through the subtle changes the inviter now has taken on the characteristics of the man he invited. The speech then comes to a most important item which the host rainhouse has and the other one surely doesn't: wine, here called the 'red serving' (*wasbid*, 'serving; a liquid dipped from a container'). Reference is then made to the guest from the distant rainhouse. He is seated before the serving and the speech says:

You swallowed it, you drank it,
Beautifully drunk, beautifully dizzy,
You didn't keep from me the good talk,
Your good dreams, good songs.

Two days after that according to the speech the east wind brought rain.

An important difference from the previous speeches is that the rains at the end are not sent by the owner of the distant 'rainhouse', but they have come from winds which 'understood and ran' after the owner of the house had gone to the host village. There has been a double shift. The host's round house has been deified, that is, described as a *wa'aki* full of wind, clouds, and seeds, plus the all important wine; and the onset of the rain has been made more in accord with "reality," that is, it comes from a distant, apparently nonhuman source ('the wind from the east understood and ran'). In this manner the poles of the first pair of speeches are brought closer together.

The 'sit and drink' proper is a complex ceremony which includes sermons, songs, and wine servings as well as two more stages of ritual oratory. The following is a sketch of the event as it is done at Santa Rosa. After the guests are seated, two men from the host village come from under the sunshade to address everyone about the seriousness and purpose of the event. This is a sermon in the sense defined in the Introduction, not a ritual oration. Next a short oration is given four times to the people sitting in the four directions (the host village sits in front of the sunshade occupying the west). This speech is missing in Underhill's collection and we do not make up for that lack. It is spoken in the order of east, south, north, and west. East is primary as this is the direction from which the summer rainstorms usually come. This fact will become more important as the book proceeds. Here we may simply note that this is the first speech of the wine feast that is specifically keyed to all four directions. Following the speech, wine is served by eight servers, all from the host village. Two servers, each with a basket of wine, go to each of the four directions. They first serve two main representatives of the village of that direction, then move around the circle (one going clockwise, the other going counterclockwise) pouring wine for each person that they come to. Each person sitting in the circle may be served three or four times, totalling between a pint and a quart, before the baskets are empty. The wine is about as strong as commercial beer. It is an emetic, that is, after drinking a quart or two it makes one vomit.

Following this first formal drinking of cactus wine, it is the turn of the people seated in each direction to sing a special song, called 'sit and drink song'. Again the order is east, south, north, and west. The leaders of these songs are the same individuals as were invited by the 'running' speeches and seated with the 'seating' speeches. Here they sing, perhaps as gods.

After the songs a second round of drinks is served. The 'sit and drink' then closes with a final round of oratory, called the 'mockingbird speeches' *(ṣu:gaj ñiok)*. Spoken four times to the four directions, this speech begins with the idea that everyone has now drunk wine—as truly they have. The speech then shifts from the here and now to a mockingbird in a distant rainhouse. According to the speech, it is the mockingbird who 'talks' and is responsible for the release of winds, clouds, and rains. With this the ceremony ends.

MOCKINGBIRD SPEECH

Jose Pancho, Santa Rosa

(TO THE EAST, SOUTH, AND NORTH)

Do:owai, na'as hemu am a s-ap'e ñ-nawoj, mapt ab ba:	Ready, seems that now it is fine my friend, now you have swallowed

Ma:kai wasib, siwañ wasib, e-o'og we:nadk ab ba:	Medicine man's liquid, rain maker's liquid, mixed with your tears you have swallowed it
Ha'akia e-ṣo'igmadag we:nadk ab ba:.	Mixed with your snot you have swallowed it.
K wa:haj ñeid g si'aligc eḍ ke:kam wa'aki mab ke:k	Far off [you] see the eastern [southern, northern] standing rainhouse that stands there
Mo g eḍa s-to:ta a'anam ṣu:g ab nagia.	Where inside the white [green, red] feathered mockingbird hangs.
O wa ip gi'ikho da'imo'otk c ñiok	Four times he bends upward and talks
Ce:khimac niok, kuawit huḍugc ñiok, a'ai da'iwanc ñiok	Jumps up and down and talks, bends downward and talks, moves back and forth and talks
Kok hia wa g jeweḍ s-wa'akpadagc hab cu'ig.	And the earth is wet.
Do:owai, ta waṣan i hoi jeweḍ hugid an, amjeḍ g hewel si s-e-ma:ck i me:	Ready, then far off something moved at the edge of the earth, the wind understood and ran
U'us cu:cim i gi:gidahim, tanahadag wakomedag i wi'um k g u'us cu:cim ab si ṣondadahim, at a hab juñhimk ab huḍunigt ab si ce:mo'o	Standing trees it [wind] shook, trash it blew and piled at their feet, it continued and arrived at the west [north, south]
Kup ta'am u:pam ha'ahogi i i-wuak cem ñei	Homeward it turned and looked
T kia jeweḍ ka:cim am a ge s-keg cu'igk na:to.	The lying earth was clean and finished.
Tag da:m ab wu:ṣ ge s-to:ta ṣoṣon am ce:wagi	On top of that came out the white [green, red] bottomed cloud
Da:m ka:cim baṣo mo'oṣc ab ke:k, ha'akia e-we:m ku:gc ab ke:k	To the top of the sky it bumped and stood, with many round ends it stood
At a wa i hi:.	And it went.
Ha'akia jegosidag, ha'akia wepogidag, ha'hakia duahimdag, ha'akia cewagig, ha'akia kiohodag, at a wa i hi:.	With many dust storms, with many lightnings, with many thunders, with many clouds, with many rainbows, it started to go.
S-wa:papagam do:da'ag e'eḍa ab da'iwonhim c ab e-we:ndahim	From within wet mountains, more [clouds] came out and joined it
Ab e-babṣo s-to:tam hu:pkim, ab e-babṣo s-to:tam ce:ceghun.	Plucking out white [green, red] from their breasts, coughing out white from their breasts.
Ka jeweḍ wa cem si s-me:kodam hogidagc ka:c	The earth seemed so far to its edge
Tag ab si hogidagcudk ba'ic ju:k cem ñei.	But they went clear to the edge and beyond and looked.
Ka wipiṣan e-a:gc c ha'akia e-honṣ we:c, hekihu um cem si mo:mo'ink e-elid	And the little washes thought of themselves that so many of them lay side by side, they can carry off anything, they thought

Kag am pi a : haidam juñhim, e-ciciñ an wapko'ola ga : kai ab i ṣa'icudahim.

At a hab juccuhimk ab si ce : mo'o
P ta'am u : pam ha'ahogi i i-wuak cem ñei
T kia jeweḍ ka : cim am ge s-keg wa'opagidk na : to.
Tag da : m ab wu : ṣ g ha'icu kaikam, ha'as ṣawaḍk tatk, ha'as ṣawaḍk wa'ok, ge s-tatañ hahak, ge s-keg ciñwodag, ge s-keg muḍadagc ke : k, ta'am s-keg bai.
Ko wa i : da hemako t-kug taccuidag c hab e-ju :
Tag am o ñei.

But it [flood] couldn't be stopped, at their mouths the driftwood piled crossways.
Thus it [storm] did and was completed
Homeward it turned and looked
The lying earth was beautifully wet and finished.
On top of that came out something seeded, thick was its root, thick was its stalk, wide was its leaf, good were its silks, good was its tassel, well did it ripen.
It was this that was our last wish and it happened
As you will see.

(TO THE WEST)

Do : wai, na'as hemu am a s-ap'e n-ñawoj, mapt ab ba :
Ma : kai wasib, siwañ wasib, e-o'og we : nadk ab ba :

Ha'akia e-ṣo'igmadag we : nadk ab ba : .

K wa : haj ñeid g huḍuñigc eḍ ke : kam wa'aki mab ke : k
Mo g eḍa s-cuk a'anam ṣu : g ab nagia.

O wa ip gi'ikho da'imo'otk c ñiok
Ce : khimac ñiok, kuawit huḍugc ñiok, a'ai da'iwanc ñiok

Kok hia wa g jeweḍ s-wa'akpadagc hab cu'ig.
Do : wai, ta waṣan i hoi jeweḍ hugid an, amjeḍ g hewel si s-e-ma : ck i me :

U'us cu : cim i gi : gidahim, tanahadag wakomedag i wi'um k g u'us cu : cim ab si ṣondadahim, at a hab juñhimk ab si'aligt ab si ce : mo'o
Kup ta'am u : pam ha'ahogi i i-wuak cem ñei
T kia jeweḍ ka : cim am a ge s-keg cu'igk na : to.
Tag da : m ab wu : ṣ ge s-cuk hikom
Ka jeweḍ a cem si s-taḍañc ka : c

Ready, seems that now it is fine my friend, now you have swallowed
Medicine man's liquid, rain maker's liquid, mixed with your tears you have swallowed it
Mixed with your snot you have swallowed it.
Far off [you] see the western standing rainhouse that stands there
Where inside the black feathered mockingbird hangs.
Four times he bends upward and talks
Jumps up and down and talks, bends downward and talks, moves back and forth and talks
And the earth is wet.
Ready, then far off something moved at the edge of the earth, the wind understood and ran
Standing trees it [wind] shook, trash it blew and piled at their feet, it continued and arrived at the east
Homeward it turned and looked
The lying earth was clean and finished.
On top of that came out the black drizzle
The earth very broadly lay

Kut ag ab a'i si hogidadcudk at a ab e-juccuhim	But it [drizzle] went back and forth at the edge and continued
Kat a ab si'aligt ab si ce:mo'o	Then at the east it arrived
Kut a am u:pam ha'ahogi i i-wuak cem ñei	Homeward turned and looked
T kia jeweḍ ka:cim am ge s-keg wa'opagidk na:to.	The lying earth was beautifully wet and finished.
Tag da:m ab wu:ṣ ge na:nko ma:s ha'icu kaikam, ge opon, ge ṣu'uwat, ge da:pk, c we:s am hugkam ho'i ke:kam, at a am ge s-keg bai.	On top of that came out various seeded things, *opon, ṣu'uwat, da:pk* [all wild greens or grasses], and every kind of cactus, well did they ripen.
Ko wa i:da hemako t-kug taccuidag c hab e-ju:	It was this that was our last wish and it happened
Tag am o ñei.	As you will see.

We see that this speech takes up roughly where the 'seating' speech left off. It emphasizes the wind that 'understood and ran'. There is no journey by a human at all in this speech. Rather, the speech concentrates on the motions set in train by the drinking of wine.

To understand them we must understand the mockingbird. Papagos know the bird as a species with no calls of its own. It merely imitates other birds. Although the speech doesn't say so in so many words, a plausible reading of the story is: The people are now drunk and celebrating. The mockingbird hears them and passes the sounds on. Through him the wind hears of the event, and it 'understands and runs'. It is ambiguous whether the bird understood and meant what he said, or simply copied the sounds. He is described as if drunk in his rain-house, with his head bobbing this way and that, as if he copied not only the sounds of the ceremony but also its mood.

The speech continues with the description of a tremendous rainstorm. Clouds bump against the sky, lightning flashes, dust storms roll across the land, the normally dry and empty washes are filled to overflowing and choked with debris. It is a glorious conclusion and just what humanity wants. The speech ends with (corn) plants coming out, forming thick stalks, wide leaves, good tassels, etc. This is the pattern of all but the westward mockingbird speech. There drizzle replaces the thunderclouds and there is no talk of a flood of water. The resulting plant growth is wild food and cactus. We will learn more about the special properties of the west in the next chapter.

The 'sit and drink' lasts about an hour. After it come several days and nights of celebration at individuals' houses. Each family has made its own supply of wine. As this wine becomes ready, it is given in baskets to invited guests. The guests seat themselves at the host's house and dispense the wine to all who gather around them. The proper response on being served is to sing songs. People eat and sleep at irregular intervals as the normal distinction between night and day has been set aside.

At the ocean. Drawing by Mike Chiago.

Ocean

In former times the Papagos got all their salt from the northeast shore of the Gulf of California. This required a week's round trip journey. The custom has declined in direct proportion to the availability of cheap salt in stores and supermarkets, so now the idea of a salt pilgrimage is remote to nearly everyone. Other oceans are now far better known than the Gulf of California, for example, the Pacific off Los Angeles, and the Atlantic that soldiers crossed in World War II. The meaning of this particular ocean in the old timers' scheme of things is one of the most intriguing questions about the ritual year.

Underhill learned that summer was the preferred time for salt pilgrimages. It would seem to be the least comfortable, being the hottest, and the journey was over extremely arid land. The reason given to her was that the high tides of spring would leave unusually large deposits of salt on the beach (1946:213). Thus we class the journey as a summer rite, falling between the rain ceremonies just considered and the hunting rites considered next. The texts of the speeches agree with this. They are divided between those that emphasize rain just as the wine feast speeches do, and those that emphasize the ocean. Ultimately it will be seen that the salt water ocean and the rain water 'rainhouses' stand in opposition to each other.

We are most fortunate to have a document on the salt pilgrimage written by a participant in journeys of a century ago. It was written in 1897 in English by Jose Lewis Brennan of *Wainom Ke:k* ('Iron Stands'), a village slightly to the south of the group whose wine feast was just discussed. The author first went to the ocean in 1879.

While written in English, Brennan's account will readily be recognized by Papagos as a Papago way of telling stories. It is formed in long sentences whose component parts (clauses) echo and build upon each other. We may be sure that its content is Papago, too.

The author wrote his account in longhand in a lined notebook. He used paragraph form. Bahr has taken the liberty to write it in lines as poetry in the belief that this method better shows the narrative style mentioned above. This is the only change that has been made. Brennan's word order, word choices, and punctuation have been faithfully retained. A very few changes have been made in spelling. If the text is read with stress on and a slight pause after the last word of each line, it will sound like what it is, the transposition of Papago oral "prose" narrative into written English. This was no mean feat on Brennan's part. It is equivalent to an artist shifting to a new medium. To achieve his purpose Brennan had to know the new medium, the writing of English, very well.

CUSTOM ON GOING FOR SALT

Jose Lewis Brennan, Wainom Ke:k

Fresnal, Quijotoa and Santa Rosa
    Papagos all believe
That the Ocean is a Supreme Being.
But as many other things today
They began gradually leaving out.
But the Ocean shall never
And will never be considered
As a common water or unworthy
    mysterious being.

It contains the idea
That the Ocean has power equal to God
And whenever wishes to destroy us
It would rise up and drown us.

So the Papagos in getting salt
Perform many ceremonies
And each man must suffer
More than it is necessary
In order so he may have a chance
To obtain some power from the Ocean
As a singer or a doctor.

They say
That sometimes a person may obtain any
    kind of power,
He may become an expert gambler,
Runner, hunter, football kicker, horse
    rider,
Or (*Svi'tipika* = one who cuts off the
    animal's testicles without hurting
    them).

I went there three times
And I never get any power or luck
And so with many others
Who constantly goes there
To get the salt.

I went there once in 1879
And twice in 1885.

When a person makes his first trip
To the gulf of lower California
To get the salt,
[He] suffers more than those others
Who have gone before.

There are but very few
Who can be a leader
In going to get the salt.
The leader must know the ceremonies of
    this kind
So he can tell all the people
Who are with him.

People going to get the salt
Must leave everything at home
That is,
He must not think anything back
After leaving his home.
Because if he do
His trip would be unsuccessful.

When a leader wants to go to get the salt
He tells the other people
And if anybody want to go with him
[He] would be very welcome.
The leader gives chance to everybody
Who desire to go
[And they] must be ready in four days.

After four days
They would left their homes
About 7-8 or 9 o'clock in the morning
And traveled maybe 40 or 60 miles
And camp.

Person who goes there for the first time
I suppose feels like a man feels
When he first converts in the Christian
life.
I know I feel like that
At the time I went there first.

Of course person has to be taught
Before he could go there
So he would not expect
To have good time
While he is on the way.
People must not talk each other
While they are going
On the road.
People are allowed only to say
One or two words
When it is necessary.

In the evenings
At the camp
People are allowed to talk only
Of the past journey
And nothing else,
Like the Christian people
When they try to convert the people
They talk or preach only
The name of Jesus Christ
And nothing else.

After maybe an hour
The leader will take out a reed
Cut six inches long
And one inch and a half circumference
And half an inch in diameter,
Fill up with tobacco.
This is call *va'pi oa'tc'ki*
Reed cigarette
Or reed cigar.

This cigarette
Lasted long time
For they use it only
In these occasions.
In olden times
They used to smoke it
When they are engaged
In war with the Apache.

After the leader
Has taken out
The cigarette
He lights it
And smoke it four times
And then pass it
To the first man
On his left.

Usually
Among the White people
When they have meetings,
The audience sits in rows
Facing to the speaker,
While
The Papago builds fire
And sits
Around in circle.

In passing the reed cigarette
Each man have to smoke it
Four times only
And then lowering slowly
Straight down from his breast
Until reached the ground
And then drag
On the ground
And hand it to the next
And so on.

If there is any
Man whose wife,
Daughter or sister
[Is] pregnant or menstruating
[He] would not smoke it
But he'll take it
And passed it
To the next man.

After the reed cigarette
Reach the leader from where it started
Then he began to repeat the speech
Which is handed down
From his ancestors
Probably thousands of years ago
And until to this day.

He says:
We are here my friends and relatives.
When I was in my house
I did not know
What I shall eat or drink,
What to think and what I shall do.

My mind was affected
And I try to find something behind my
housepost
And around my fireplace, under my
pillow
And I did not find anything.

But at last I found a stump of my
cigarette:
I stir the ashes, but the fire was dead.
I took a piece of wood in my fireplace,
I saw that the fire was indeed extinct.
But yet I blow at it and its blaze came,
Then I light my cigarette stump
And I smoke it.

I was then know
How to think and what to do.
It was the power of my reed cigarette
stump
Which I smoked and it give me light,
And I see that my land was barren,
My mountain stands without clouds on
their tops,
The trees without leaves,
The animals of the land and of the
mountains
Lost their senses,
The birds and fowls of the air
Forgotten their cries and songs.
I see that the wind, clouds and rain
Are shut up themselves
In the east, north, south and west.
But it was the power of my reed cigarette
stump
Which I smoked,

I arose
And went to the east making four slides
And get there,
I see that the wind, cloud and rain were
fasten up,
Tied with cords.
It was impossible for me to open and talk
with them.
But it was the power of my cigarette
stump
Which I smoked and it was open.

After it has been open I see
That the wind, cloud and rain were
sitting
With their faces the other way.
But it was the power of my cigarette
stump
Which I smoked and make them turn
their faces toward me.
Then I began telling them about my
country and the looks thereof,
Why [did] they shut up themselves,
Leaving us with the desire for wind and
rain.
When I end my request, they said
Go and wait four days
And your wishes will be accomplished.

I turned around and made four slides
And reached my fireplace
Where I waited four days,
And it seems to be a very long time
When it does come the four days.
After four days I see that the wind
seemed to blow good,
The clouds and the rain with lightning,
thunders, and rainbows.
The rain came reaching the outermost
part of the North and South,
Reached the West,
And then the rain from the North
reached the South
And from the South reached the North
And from the West reached the East.

All this was done and I was glad and said
to my sons,
Go, and whatever you see come back and
tell us about it,
And they went away.

When they got back the first one said
—Father, I went across the valley

I saw the ground was swelling up
And in some places the grass was up and many other things.
When I come up to the hills and the cactus fruits was also coming up.
The second one said
—Father, when I left the house
I went across the valley
I saw that the grass, trees, cactus and other things were growing
And big enough to eat.
The active woman hear these news
And she wouldn't sleep good,
While there was not yet morning she got up
And looking east but there was no sign of daylight.
But the night soon pass and the morning come,
She put on her fastest walking shoes and her *giha* [carrying basket]
And went away.
When she got to the place where the cactus were big enough to be use
She soon filled her *giha* and got back
And the old man was talking about,
So you may think of that my friends and relatives.

This speech is also used in olden times
When they make war against the Apaches.

After when the leader closes his speech
Or finishes repeating of this speech,
Then everyone addresses him by the term of expression
Of the relationship between them.

After this is done,
Then the leader will tell them
Why these rules have to be followed,
And encourage them not to think that this is a hard task,
But to think that this is only one day suffering
And that is all.

After they talked a while and smoke,
Then the leader tells them to bring their pinole
So he can give them something to eat
Before they go to bed.

The leader gives each man one grip or handful of pinole
And each man receives as much as the other
And they put water in it and stir it up
And let it stay a while until settled down,
They they drink only the top
And when come to the thickest
Each man makes a little hole in the ground
And poured in
And put a little dirt.

After [that]
They go to bed.
Usually
When they are many
[They] build fires
In groups of 4 or 5
In each fire.

Early in the morning
Just as soon as daybreak
[The] leader calls out and
Everybody have to run to get his pony.
No person is allowed to walk
In getting his horse or anything,
Must run,
No matter how near anything he may get,
Whether [they] are three or four feet from him
He must run and run back
Like lightning.

Nobody have right to go ahead of the leader.
Leader must see at camp
That everybody gets ready
Before he mounts his horse.
So when everybody gets ready
Then he gets on his pony

And go on the road
And the rest of them have to follow him
Up close to,
Nobody is allowed to fool far behind,
People must keep up with the others.

It takes maybe 50 or 60 miles journey
In the morning
Before anybody can expect to have
breakfast.
The food which they carried
For their provision is pinole [cooked
flour],
Each man carry food and water
But he have no right
To eat or drink
Until he is given [it]
By the leader
With the rest of the party.

They have two meals [a] day,
One at 11 o'clock A.M.
And the other
After the meeting or ceremonies.
At 11 o'clock A.M. they stop
And make the horse rest a while.
Everybody have to set down
With his face to the direction he is going.
There they cut they cut
The sacred head scratcher [*kus ko't.*].

There are two other speeches
Besides this I have written
And it is much alike.

The second night,
The leader will act the same as the first
night.
The leader tells once more the people
About the customs and rules
How each man must persevere
While engaged in gathering the salt.
He prescribes especially that night
Because next day will be at the salt field.

He forbid every man
To let everything alone and
If [he] so desire
To get anything in the ocean or gulf
[He] must ask blessings
From the ocean or gulf
Before taking it
And must bring it to me
So I may put the *tcoi-i* [flour] on.

After the meeting is over
The leader tells them to bring their
pinole
So he can give supper
And after supper
Then they all go to bed
For a little while.

About an hour from that time
When the leader calls out
And everybody would be running
Here and there.

In a few minutes
Everybody gets ready
And travel again
In the night
And about daybreak
They will see a sand hill,
They would run their horses up to the hill
And stop on the top
About 15 minutes
The leader will repeat a short speech
Which I could never hear,
Because breathing of the horses.

For a while only
And then they go again.

About 7 or 8 o'clock A.M.
The the leader stops and tell all the other
people
To get ready for the horse race
From there to the well.

The well is about 2 or 3 miles from the
salt field,
And from the well to where they are
Must be about 20 miles.

When everybody gets ready
The leader repeats another short speech,
And as soon as he stops his speech,
Everybody starts.

In arriving at the well
Every man have to run his horse
Around the well once
And if the horse has never been there
He runs it around four times
And then he water it.

At the well
Every man
Takes his pants off
And put on the breech-clout only.

When they get to the salt field
And those who have been there before
Have to run around
The salt field once,
While those whose first trip,
Must run around four times.

The salt field is one mile around.
After that they gather the salt
From 10 o'clock A.M.
To 2 o'clock P.M.
The they put in the sacks
And make it ready
For the next day to come back.

This is call Salt-harvest,
But the people
Who are engaged in gathering the salt,
Says [corn-harvest].

All the plants
As cactus, trees and other bushes
They call weed and
The animals birds and fowls,
They call men or people.

At two o'clock P.M. then
They have their meal or breakfast.
And rest one hour.

After this the leader will tell them
Why these rules have to be followed.
The leader says
That it is better
For anyone to suffer
Just as much as person desire,
Because the Ocean will not dispose
Any man's life.
Although two men were dead and buried
Near the salt field,
Caused of much exertion
Just because the leader tells them
To do so
Or maybe that these people expect to
receive some power
From the Ocean,
But they just kill themselves.

At three o'clock P.M.
The leader will give each man
A little flour
In his left hand
And in the crowd
[To] one of the fastest runner
The leader will give a stick to him
And the stick is the size of a lead pencil,
Sharp on one end
And four inches long.

This man
Who carry the stick
Leads all the others.

They will run
From there to the beach,
Each man have to go down
On right hand side
Of the person who carry the stick.

Every man takes his flour
And go in where the waves comes up,
They throw [a] little
In the waves four times
And if [there] is any left
They threw all in the water.

After each person get through
He runs westward by the beach
As far as he wishes.

The man
Who carried the stick
Puts it in the waves
After asking a good luck
For everyone.

All those who wished to
Run far west
He never looked back but
As soon he look back
He can't go any farther,
He have to turned around
And go home.

Many people
Are just run for miles and
Never get any power
From the Ocean.
I suppose there are but very few
Who make their luck and become
somebody
Or know something.

When almost everybody gets home
The leader will call a short meeting
And then tells them
To bring their pinole
So he can give them their supper
And then go to bed.

If any body absent
The leader will stay up or set up to see
That every body come home
Before he go to bed.

In leaving the salt field
At 8 or 9 o'clock A.M.
People will put their minds to their
homes
And no person will think anything back
Or neither look back.

Before they left at the salt field
The leader will repeat a short speech
While the others will stand by the salt
bags
And soon as the leader stops talking
They put the bags of sacks
On the horses and go
While the leader waits and see that every
body go on
Before he follows them up
Way behind.

In leaving the salt field,
They have breakfast early,
And every body
Have to walk home from there.

From 8 o'clock A.M. to 4 o'clock P.M.
They rest a while and have their supper.
Here is the only place where [it] is
allowed
That each man should eat all the pinole
That is given to him.
In some other places
Each man
Have to drink the water only
And soon [as] he comes to the thickest
part
What is settled down
He have to threw away.

After an hour they would left again
And traveled all that evening
And part of the night
About 9 or 10 o'clock P.M.
Reach the camping place
And then camp.

People have to go to bed
Soon as they put their horses in good
places
Where are lots of grass
So the horses can have plenty to eat.

In about two hours
From that time
The leader will call out
And every body would be up
And in a few minutes they would be off
again
While the leader waits
Until every body goes on the he follows
them up.

All that night until 7 o'clock A.M.
They arrive at the water place
And stay there
And cut a new sacred head scratcher
[*kus-ko't*].

Then
At 11 o'clock A.M.
They have their breakfast
And at one o'clock P.M.
They starts again.

All that afternoon
To 9 o'clock at night they camp
And there they have meeting
And the leader encourage,
Telling them the same thing
He has been already told them.

After two or three hours
The leader then tell them
To bring their pinole
So he can give them a supper and
Then go to bed.

In about two hours from that time
The leader calls out so
Every body at once be up and
In a few minutes,
They would be off again.
As it is the custom
That the leader should wait and see
That all go on
Then he follows them up.

At 7 or 8 o'clock A.M.
They stops at some water
Then every man takes bath and stay there
Until in the afternoon
Then they go again.
Considering that next day will be
At home.

They may camp early
About 6 o'clock in the evening
And spend their time in running,
To breathe out the smell of the Ocean.

In the night
The leader will tell them
How the old people used to do
And tell how each man must do
When he gets home
And many other things
The leader describes,
Advise them because it is danger.

Those who have wives
Should and must not go with their wives
On the arrival
And as long as his term extend
And until he complete the time
That the leader may give them.

This meeting will last
Almost the whole night
All that time
There be many sleeping and not listening
Because they are tired and hungry.

But at last
The leader will tell them
To bring their provision.
He will give each man
The same proportion as usually.
Each person receives
As much as the other.

Here the leader
Will give permission
To the old people only
To eat all the pinole
That which is given to them.

After this then
They all go to bed.

Next day
They would not start early
Until after sun rise
And then they go again.

When they get near to their village
About two miles from there
They stop and the leader
Will repeat a short speech

And then every man mounts his horse
And go.

When they get to their homes.
The mother or wife,
Sees her boy or husband,
She would cry,
Because the person would lost
His beauty.
Because he becomes poor like
As if he has been sick
For two or three months.

After that
His salt is unload,
Take his saddle bag off
The he sits down
With his face
To the direction
He just came
And reviews his trip in his mind
From the starting point
To the salt field
Then his return
To where he is sitting.

By that time
His breakfast will be ready
What is call *atole*,
Made of corn meal
Into a thin soup.

After he drink it,
He lay down
And go to sleep.

His mother or wife
Will cook something
Of the very best she can find,
And by that time
There will be a man running on
horseback
Telling all the people
To come and sing for these people
Who has just returned
From the salt field and
This is call *hew-'fitco-lita*.

In the evening each man
Those who brought the salt,
Have to bring it
About 5 or 10 pounds
And put it in a basket
For those people who are going to sing for
them
And for the others also.

The food is given
To each of the singer.

Big fire is built
In front of the chief's house
Or *Djer-nu'k-'tcuk-tcim*
And the men
Those who returned from the salt field
Will sit in a curve line
About 20 feet away from the fire
On the south side.

The singers will sit in the northwest,
The ahead singer will sit at west side
Also 20 feet from the fire.

When they gather at the chief's house
And before they begin singing,
One of them will repeat the same speech
Which is already written.
There are two other speeches similar to
the one written
And the other two which I am not
familiar with,
That is,
I have not heard often
So I don't know.

After that they begin singing
And each singer have two sticks
One larger holding on his left hand,
Cut like a saw,
And the other smaller on the right hand
Running it forward and backward
On where it is cut like a saw.

Every fourth song they stop
And go to the men
Where are sitting
In curve line
And with the two sticks
Touching them saying
That they should have good luck
And become doctors or runners &c.
The whole night.

Next day
The salt that was collected
By those who brought the salt,
Will be divided among them.

The people who brought the salt
Will then count the days
From that time on
That [the] leader gave them to live
Separate from his family.

All that time
He eat or drinks only the *atole*
Twice a day,
Mornings and evenings
And every four days,
He takes a good bath.

When his term is expire
Then he can go in,
In his house and eat
Whatever he wishes to.

This is the custom in going for salt
And it is a disgrace for anyone to stay at home
Who is big enough or old enough
To stand the thirst or hunger
And other sufferings.
Sometimes a man may get a bad name
For not going with the people for salt.

The reader who followed this account correctly knows that the journey covered seven days and six nights. The night after the arrival home was filled with celebration—the singing of what Brennan spelled as *hew-'fitco-lita*, which we would now write as *hewculida*, 'scraping' songs. Counting the time in preparation before the journey and the purification after it, the salt pilgrimage required 15 days and 16 nights (Table 4).

Nights are as important as days in Brennan's telling. Sometimes there was traveling through the night and often there were ceremonies. Periods of rest come as often in the day as in the night. In short and like the wine feast discussed in the previous chapter, once a ritual is set in motion, the normal routine of work in the day and sleep in the night is suspended. A new kind of time is in force—for half a month in this case. We may call it "ritual time."

For the feelings and other details of the ritual, the document can speak for itself. We may note that Underhill's findings on the salt pilgrimage agree with Brennan in all important respects. She was told of two different routes to the ocean, one which took two and a half days (the same as Brennan), the other which took four (1946:215). Ak Chin village used the first route, Santa Rosa and Anegam used the second one. These are the three villages from which her information came. Her chapter on the salt pilgrimage includes information not found in or differently stressed in Brennan's account. Both should be read to get the full picture. Our interest now, however, is in the speeches that she collected.

This book's best proof of the integrity of oratory through time and space is the close relation between the speech in Brennan from the 1880s and two of the five salt speeches collected by Underhill in the 1930s, one from Anegam and one

TABLE 4

NIGHTS AND DAYS OF THE SALT PILGRIMAGE

Night	Announce upcoming journey
Day	Preparations
Night	
Day	
Night	
Day	
Night	
Day	
Night	
Day	Travel 40 miles
Night	Camp, ceremonies
Day	Travel 50 miles, cut head scratchers, ceremonies
Night	Rest one hour. Arrive at sand hill, ceremonies
Day	Race to well, arrive at ocean, gather salt, throw flour
Night	Sleep at ocean
Day	Depart from ocean
Night	Rest two hours, then travel
Day	Arrive at well, rest until afternoon. Travel from afternoon until dark
Night	Rest two hours, then travel until morning
Day	Rest until afternoon, then travel
Night	Hold meeting and sleep
Day	Arrive at village, rest during the day
Night	Celebration of return
Day	Give out salt, beginning of journeyers' "term" (purification)
Night	
Day	
Night	
Day	
Night	
Day	
Night	End of journeyers' "term"

from Santa Rosa. According to her information the two speeches were used on different nights in the four day trek to the ocean, one on the second night and one on the last. There are problems with this itinerary as presented in *Papago Indian Religion.*[1] In any case the two speeches are quite like each other and quite like Brennan's. Two of her remaining speeches, one each from Anegam and Santa Rosa, are also quite alike. We will call them type "A" speeches and type "B" speeches and temporarily leave aside the question of which came first. Her fifth

[1]It is stated that one was used on the second night, that one was used on the last night, that the second speech was used when 'Black Mountain' was climbed (a place corresponding to the sandy hill in the itinerary followed by Brennan), and that there was a two day journey along the coast subsequent to the ceremonies at Black Mountain. This accounting of nights, places, and speeches has contradictions.

speech, from Santa Rosa, was used in the celebration of the return and will be presented as type "C." Let us begin by summarizing the Brennan oration which is of type "A."

Preface: The hero was in his house. He found his cigarette stump, lit it, and smoked it. This lighted the world so he could see its pitiable condition.

Body, Part I: He arose, went eastward, and reached a place where wind, rain, and clouds were tied up so they couldn't move. His cigarette smoke caused them to untie themselves and to face him. He asked them to water the land and they said that they would.

Body, Part II: He returned home and waited four days.

Conclusion: Wind, clouds, and rain crisscrossed the world. The hero sent his two sons to see the results. They returned with good reports. Then the active woman went out to gather fresh cactus fruit.

The Anegam version of this speech has a larger body with more *parts* but its story is essentially the same: a search for the cigarette, a journey to the east, arrival at a house wrapped with clouds and rainbows, and the release of rains after the hero smokes and talks with the "owner" of the house, here referred to by the word 'made father', *o:gta*.[2] The difference between this speech and Brennan's is that it says relatively more about the hero's journeying while Brennan says relatively more in his concluding section about what happened after the hero returned. It is a question of different emphasis within the overall plan of an oration as given in the Introduction of this book.

SALT PILGRIMAGE SPEECH "A"

Jim Thomas (Dionisio), Anegam

Ko wa hascu bahijidk am cem ñ-ma:	There was something they cooked and tried to give me
Ṣu:dagi wasibk am cem ñ-ma:	Water they dipped and tried to give me
Nt am pi i: ka hab i ñ-a:g	But I didn't drink and they said to me
"Ṣa:cu wuḍ hems has e-ju:	"What could have happened
S hemu ia pi i-hug ha'icu ñ-bahijidda	Now you don't eat my cooking
Ṣu:dagi ñ-wasib ia pi e-i:"	Water that I dipped you don't drink"
Bo wa ñ-a:g	I thought
"Ñ-ha'ap abṣ ñ-ta:tk."	"I just feel like that."

[2]Underhill translates this term, *o:gta*, as 'guardian.' Its literal meaning is 'made father.' It is a term of ritual kinship. Individuals addressed by this term respond to the addressor with the word *cu:cuḍ*, 'younger sibling's child.'

A translation as 'guardian' is legitimate because the Papago concept of *o:gta* is part of the widespread "guardian spirit" complex of Native North America. We use the term 'made father' to draw attention to the particularity of the Papago concept which, so far as the materials in this book are concerned, takes two forms. It is used in ritual purifications or initiations where the 'made father' is a flesh and blood human; and it is used in ritual orations where the 'made father' is either Coyote or a "god" who dwells at some distance from normal human society. The first form is documented only for the war campaign. The second form occurs in the oratory for salt pilgrimages and for war.

I

Nt ha'ap am wu:ṣ,
Ta am ṣaṣdkam oidk i himhi, ia ta'ataj

G je:jeg oidk ne:nhog hab cem ñ-wuihim
Nt a ha'ap ñ-juccuhim.
Nt a hebai g u:s ap'ecudk weco am kupal hejel ñ-wua
Nt a no:nhoi si ka:kiobink tua, kuawuk wo'iwa.
Ka wuḍ hemako wi'ikam oks
Ta hebai ha'icu s-ma:cok
An cem s-ba:bagi e-a:g
O wa g am s-ñ-a:gidam kaij.
Nt a am ñ-da:gṣk i wam
Nt a ñ-wuhio mawua
Nt a g jeweḍ am i dagkwa
Nt a g ñ-mo'o eḍa mawua
Nt a g tanhadag gi:gim.

I

I set out
Went among scattered plants, trying to hide behind them
Went among open places trying to look
Thus I continued
Somewhere found a good tree and below it face down threw myself
Crossed my arms and put them down, put my forehead down.
There was one ancient woman
Somewhere she had learned something
Slowly she told it
Wanting to tell me she spoke.
I pressed down and arose
Touched my face
Rubbed off the dirt
Touched my hair
Shook out the trash.

II

Nt a am wu:ṣ
K ant am ai g ñ-watto
Nt ag eḍa am cem dahiwa
Pi am hu wuḍ hegai
Nt a am ba'ic hab iñ-ju:.
Nt a am ñ-ki:jig am ñ-kawickkadk
Wan da'am ñ-wo'ikuḍ eḍ cem wo'iwa
Pi am hu wuḍ hegai.
Nt a ab ñ-we:gaj mawua
Nt a ab ñ-biṣbadag mawup
Nt a ha'icu ga:g g ñ-uacki ton
Nt a am ba'ic hab iñ-ju:.
K am ñ-ki:kio eḍ cem mauṣa
Nt a am ba'ic hab iñ-ju:.
K ab ñ-ki:kio ṣoṣon ab cem huanahi g ñ-uacki ton
Nt a am pi nako.
Nt a am ñ-ki: s-eḍawuicudk i ba:ñhim

K hascu cecendag e-a:g

C o wa g s-tohadkam iagta a:gc e-wepogid
Nt a amjeḍ kuawid i dagiumahim
Nt a g ṣoṣon am i cem huanahi g ñ-uacki ton

II

I set out
Reached my sun shade
In that sat down
Yet that wasn't it
I had more to do.
In my [house] door I crouched
On my bed I lay
Yet that wasn't it.
I felt around myself
On my [house] wrappings I felt
Searched for my reed cigarette
I had more to do.
In my brush house tried to feel
I had more to do.
At my brush house base searched for my cigarette
But couldn't find it.
There in the middle of the house I crawled
Something should have been the house post
But it looked like a white prayer stick

Down it I slid my hands
At its base searched for my cigarette

Nt a am pi nako.
Nt a am behi g komalig ñ-gi : ki
Nt a hekaj ciock
Nt a am si ñ-kawickkadk wu : ṣ.
Nt a cem ñeid g ñ-mamtaidag mu'i
si'iṣpulk
Ki a hekihu wa i si kawpka
Hekihu i si da : dk.
Nt a am dahiwak heg hekaj i hainahim
Nt ag eḍa haspk ju : k ce : g ñ-uacki ton

T ki a eḍa hekihu wa i cem si wakumagi si
da : dk.
Nt a ab i hukwink cem ñei k o kia ab
ka : c.
Nt a am ñ-hugid am i ñei k ab wuicud
C wo'o g ma : kai ku : cki wi'idag

Ki a hekihu wa i t am si wakumagi
Hekihu i si ki : kck
Nt a behi
K am gi'igko si ṣa : mud
Ta am e'eḍa betañ
K si siwud mehi.
Ag ab ke : ṣ
K ab wa : mc
Ck hasko cem wuihim g ñ-taccui
"Ṣa : ko ont hu'i we : peg o i i : bheiwa?"

III

Nt a am si'alig wui i : pheiwa
Ka wuḍ ñ-uacki ku : bdag
S-totam e-waupan
Nt ag oid am hab iñ-juccuhim.
Kunt a gi'ik ṣoṣ
K ab ce : mo'o g si'aligc eḍ ke : kam
wa'aki.
K ab ta-ho : ho'idam cu'ig
Ha'akia s-to : ta cewagikaj e-ma'iṣ
Ha'akia kikihoḍ eḍa ga : ghai waopan
Hewelhogid an da : m gi'ikpa wu : pul
Pi has ta-do : dam cu'ig.
Ka wuḍ ñ-uacki ku : bdag
Tag hekaj am si wu : lokahim
K am si ba : bagi kuacki cem ñeid g cioj
ñ-o : gta
K am hu si ju : ko ñiac daha.

But couldn't find it.
Then took my hoe
Used it as a cane
Bent myself over and came out.
Looked at my ashes piled up

Already all hardened
Already all cracked.
Sat and with it [hoe] broke them
Inside did something and found my
cigarette
It was already rotten and cracked.

Scratched it and saw it [tobacco] was still
there.
To the side I looked and faced
There lay the medicine man's burning
stick
Already very rotten
Already full of holes
I took it
Four times shook it
Then inside it thundered
And shiningly burned.
I stood it
Puffed it
And prepared to send my wishes
"What will I first breathe out?"

III

I breathed to the east.
It was my cigarette smoke
Whitely stretching
I followed it.
I made four stops
And reached the east standing rainhouse.

Pleasant it was
With many white clouds covered
Many rainbows inside crisscrossed
Winds on top were four times tied
Not for mistreating it was.
It was my cigarette smoke
That really untied it
Slowly peeped in to see the man my made
father
Facing the other way he looked and sat.

Ka wuḍ ñ-uacki ku:bdag
Am wui si bijimit
Ab ki:jig wui ṣel ñeicudk daṣwa.

Am a ha wa a:gid
"Ṣa:pt hems cu'is cioj ñ-o:gta
Gamai g ñeid g jeweḍ m-ce:kidalig, gamai ṣo'ig ma:s
Da:m g do:da'ag m-cu:cwa, si mo:hmoñig e-cu:cwa
Da:m g u:s m-ke:ṣa, pi ha:hakc ke:k

Da:m g u'uhig m-da'icuda, k eḍa si ṣo'ig ta:hadam ṣaṣehim, am a ha wa g e-ku:ku'im pi mai
Da:m g jeweḍo melcuda, heg ṣont ab golwindahim, e-hihinki pi mai

Da:m ṣo'igkam hemajkamcuda, ha'icu s-keg hugi pi ñeid," b añ a:gid.

Ta am e'eḍa si o:m
"Heu'u cu:cuḍ, na aps hemu ia wa n-ki:eḍ, ha'icu ñ-a:gid
S-e:bid o g o'odham, pi heḍai ia hu wa:k e-elid, pt hemu ia wa:k ñ-a:gid

T hab o wa pi o ḍ si ha'icu, pegi, pt an o i ñeidkaicud, pt hebai ep a g ñ-ki:, an b a ha wo cu'igkad."
T ab haha wa baṣo maowak wo:poi ha'icu kai
S-to:ta kaikam, s-cehedagi kaikam, s-wepgi kaikam, s-da:dpk kaikam, am aha wa kawoḍkadk bei.

IV

K am hab da'iwuṣ, cem ñeid
Jeweḍ s-kuiwodam e-ce:
K oi hebai jegko ab oidk i:bheiwa g hewel
Heg eḍa gam hu i hoi an si'alig ṣoṣon an cewagi
Ab e-babṣo wepgi, ab i toahim.

Jeweḍ cem s-taḍañk e-elid
An gahi gei wi:ñim, t ab e-ṣi:sc i hi:

It was my cigarette smoke
Towards him it circled
To the door it turned his look and set him.
Then [I] said to him
"What did you do, man my made father
Look at the earth you put down, pitiful it is
On it are the mountains you stood, now crumbling they stand
On them are the trees that you stood, now leafless they stand
On them are the birds that you threw, now how sadly they fly, their cooing having forgotten
On top are the animals, there at the base [of the tree] they scratch, their howling having forgotten
On top are the poor people, something good to eat they can not see," I told him.
Inside himself he cracked
"Yes nephew, so now you have entered my house, you tell me something
The people are afraid, nobody thinks to come in here, now you come in and tell me something
But it is not difficult, so, you will look for it, someday you'll reach my home again, and it will be there."
Then he touched his chest and took away some seeds
White seeds, green seeds, red seeds, glossy seeds, then [I] bunched them up and took them.

IV

Then [I] jumped out, looked
The earth downhill lay
Then somewhere in the open breathed the wind
Far off started to move an east based cloud
On its front was lightning, there was thunder.
The earth thought it was very wide
It crossed it to the north, fastened it there and came

Ta aigo gahi gei wakliuw, t ab e-si:ṣc i hi:.	It crossed back to the south, fastened it there and came.
Ka hascu wopoṣan e-a.g c ha'akia e-hohonṣc we:c	The large washes thought of themselves that so many of them lay side by side
Ṣu:dagi ga hu a'ai e-ce:cowakhim	[But] water spilled all over them
Ka hascu wipiṣan e-a:g, ha'akia e-honṣc ka:c	The small washes thought of themselves that so many of them lay side by side
Heg oidk ṣu:dagi e-gi:gidahim.	Along them water was shaking.
Ka in hu wuḍ a'i cu:cim ma:makai-do:da'ag, da:m da'iwuñim	There were the both side standing medicine man mountains, on top of them it [cloud] came out
Ab e-we:ndahim, am hab i e-juccuhim, am ce:mo'o g huḍun ṣoṣon	Joined together, continued, reached the base of the west
Ab u:hum ha'ahog i e-wuak cem ñeid	There turned around and looked
Jeweḍ pi wahidam do:dak heg am g s-keg ñ-taccui ku:g.	The earth was spongy and there my good desire ended.
Ha'apk hems o elid na:nko ñ-i:mik.	Thus you may wish, my various relatives.

Both speeches, it may be noted, resemble the wine drinking speeches in that they result in a rainstorm. The Santa Rosa type "A" speech shares this trait while the type "B" speeches have quite a different content. Before taking up this other type of speech, let us review how rain is produced or obtained in all the speeches that we have seen so far.

The key to getting rain in these speeches is in getting an audience at a 'rainhouse' *(wa'aki)*. These houses, located at the cardinal directions, are covered with the accompaniments of rain—winds, clouds, and rainbows. In every case someone's words are needed to get the rains detached from the rainhouse and in motion across the world. In most of the speeches the words are spoken by a human hero who travels to the house. They are spoken to a mysterious person, a "rain god" who at first sits with his back to the traveler. In the ocean speeches the critical factor in turning the god around is tobacco smoke. The hero had to find his tobacco prior to setting out. The wine speeches never mention tobacco explicitly. In them the hero has to make wine before setting out. But we may equate the 'shining road' of the wine feast speeches with tobacco smoke. The Anegam salt speech just quoted clinches that interpretation for it has the hero follow his smoke like a road. In short, tobacco both helps the hero find his way and helps make his presence felt on arrival at the rainhouse. We wonder if he could have achieved his purpose without it.

The mockingbird speech of the wine feast shows a tobaccoless way to obtain rain. But it is also a journeyless way. No hero travels to a rainhouse. There is no need for a tobacco smoke 'road'. Instead of a rain god in the rainhouse, there is the mockingbird talking as if drunk. As was indicated in the previous chapter, we understand that the bird's "words," which are always in imitation of somebody else, set the rain in motion. The mockingbird replaces the hero, tobacco, and rain god of the other speeches.

We take up next a type "B" speech from Santa Rosa. It is concerned with getting grants of power rather than with making it rain. The journey is to the west rather than to the east, an opposite direction and a different outcome. It is recalled from Brennan that getting power was one of the reasons for going to the ocean. That is what this speech is about. The donor is a 'made father'. Very probably, had Brennan been able to hear the speech that was drowned out by the breathing of horses after the run up the sand hill, he would have heard a type "B" speech.

SALT PILGRIMAGE SPEECH "B"

Jose Moreno, Santa Rosa

Ko wa ha'ap masma ñ-taccuidag	This is the story of my desire
Kunt a wa g ñ-uwiga ha'icu bahijta pi ba : bagi ab hu :	There was my wife's cooking that I didn't carefully eat
Ñ-alidag pi ba : bagi ab ko : mc	My child that I didn't carefully hold
"Ṣa : cu ḍ hegai si ma : ck hab e-wua?"	"What does he know that he acts this way?"
Ta id oidk g ñ-si'alita am ce : mo'o mant am o hi : .	Through this my days were completed and so I could go.

I	I
Do : wai, nt a am wu : ṣañk ab keiṣ g huḍuñig ka : cim wo : g	Done, I emerged and stepped on the west lying road
Ta hegai si'acuk da : m ab huḍuñig wua	Someplace got tired and evening came
T am wa : m i to'a ñ-kucki wi'idag	Then took my burning stick
Am na : dk wui mu : giakc am daha	Made a fire and towards it bent over and sat
Ñ-hoaṣom eḍ maowa, am bei g ñ-uacki ton	In my bag reached and took my reed cigarette
Ab ke : ṣk ab wamṣ, am si i : bheiwa g huḍuñig ka : cim wo : g	Stood it and puffed it, breathed on the west lying road
Ab si tai g cioj ñ-o : gta.	Asked for the man my made father
Ab si tai g na : nko cu'igkam gewkdag	Asked for different kinds of strength
Bihugstalig, kustalig, hewostalig, s-cu-u'adahimkam ka : kio, s-ta : tkam no : nhai, s-ma : ms wu : pui.	Hungerness, thirstness, coldness, strong carrying legs, strong arms, clear eyes.

II	II
Gi'ikho iawa g i himdam ma : sidagk ep keiṣ g huḍuñig ka : cim wo : g	Four times spilled the coming dawn and again [I] stepped on the west lying road
Tam aha wa ce : mo'o g cioj ñ-o : gta	Then reached the man my made father
Tam aha wa si wa : m ñ-ju : .	Strongly to me he did

Ge s-tohama wa:g am ce:, s-toha bid wepodag, hekaj ab ñ-baṣo si cegṣat, ñ-otko ep ñ-cegṣat, ab ñ-gegkio s-cu'ucusidk a'ai si ñ-cegṣat	The white mixture he put, the white clay likeness, with it on my chest he really marked, on my back he marked me, on my shoulder blades both sides he marked me
Am aha wa si s-keg ñ-wusotk hab iñ-ju:	Then very well blew on me and did to me
Heg hekaj hab pi hebai ha'icu ta:tkc oimmeḍ.	So I would never feel things while going around.
Ha'apk hems o wa i elid na:nko ñ-i:mig.	Thus you may wish, my various relatives.

Next we give the type "A" Santa Rosa speech, which is about an eastward journey for the purpose of releasing rain. Again it is cigarette smoke which turns a 'made father' *(o:gta)* around and prompts him to release clouds that were tied around his rainhouse. The two *parts* in the body of this speech are exactly parallel to the two parts of the Brennan speech, and the language in the concluding section, about the rain, is nearly identical with the Santa Rosa mockingbird speech.

SALT PILGRIMAGE SPEECH "A"

Jose Moreno, Santa Rosa

Ko wa wuḍ s-wi'e ka:cim ha'icu taccuidagk pi nako	There was a mysterious desire that couldn't succeed
Kunt o wa ñ-cecendag we:pik mauṣpihimk pi nako	On my house post I felt, and couldn't succeed
Gi'ikho we:pik i cem maupṣik pi nako	Four times felt and couldn't succeed
Wuḍ u:s ṣopol i wi'idag, hekaj am ciowikahim ki:jigk am wu:ṣ.	There was a short stick remnant, with it I leaned in the door and came out.
Am ki:jig o g ñ-mamtaidag si si'iṣpulk, nt a hekaj am i gewaihmu	In the door my ashes were piled, with it [stick] I stirred them
Nt a am bei g ñ-uacki ton	Picked up my cigarette
Ko wa pi ab hu s-ka:cima cu'ig, nt a ab hukiwink ñeid.	It looked like it [tobacco] was not there, but I scratched it and saw [that it was there].
Ab a ka:c ab hugid ab g kucki wi'idag, s-cukc ka:c nt a gi'ikho ob si ṣoṣoñhi.	Next to it lay the burning stick, blackly lying, I four times hit it.
T ab si siwud, ge'egc mehi, nt a ab ke:ṣk ab wamc	It shined, it strongly burned, I stood it and puffed
Ka s-ku:bdagc hab cu'ig.	And smokey it was.
Ta am si'alig wui si s-oiwicik ge s-to:tam e-waopan	Eastward it [smoke] hurried, whitely it stretched
Si'alig ton ce:mo'o.	It reached the light of the east.
I	I
Nt a heg oidk hab iñ-ju:	I followed it
Ab ce:mo'o g si'aligc eḍ ke:kam wa'aki	Reached the east standing rainhouse

Ha'akia cewagicud ke:kc ab wupuli, ko ha'am pi has ñ-do:dam cu'ig.	Many clouds stood tied to it, it did not look easy for me.
Ka wuḍ cioj ñ-o:gta, si ku:kam ñiac daha.	There was the man my made father, facing the other way he looked and sat.
Ka wuḍ ñ-uacki kubdagk ha am we:big bijimhimk ñ-wui ne:ncudk daṣwa.	It was my cigarette smoke, around him it circled, towards me it turned his look and sat him.
"Ṣa: t hems e-ju: cioj ñ-o:gta?	"What has happened, man my made father?
Gamai si ṣo'ig ma:sc ka:c g jeweḍ	Over there the earth is pitiful
U:s m-ke:ṣa, pi ha:hakc ke:k	Trees that you stood, all leafless stand
U'uhig m-da'icud, heg ab cem ṣa'iwa, e-ku:ku'im pi ma:c	Birds that you threw, they just stick on them [trees], their cooing having forgotten
Ṣoṣongam ṣu:dagi am si huhu, jeweḍo meḍdam e-hihinki am pi ma:c."	The water springs are dry, the animals have forgotten their howls."
"Aheu'u cu:cuḍ, nat heg ge s-ahimk hab o e-ju:.	"Yes nephew, that came to pass and happened.
D o ki hema'ipk ha'icu wuḍ a:ga kc hab cu'ig	It was someone else's intention that happened
Gamai si ma:cok gamai u:pam hab o i e-ju:."	Later you will know this, so you can return."
II	II
Nt a am u:pam iñ-wua	I turned towards home
Huḍuñig wui jeweḍ si s-kuiwodam e-ju:, ta heg oidk am s-ba:babi hab iñ-ju:	Westward the land was sloped down, along it I slowly went
Ce:mo'o g ñ-wo'ikuḍ	Reached my bed
Ta am gi'ik g ñ-si'aligac ha am ce:mo'o.	Four times my mornings were completed.
Wuḍ a si'alig tagiojeḍ hewel, si s-e-ma:ck i me:	There was the east wind, it really knew and ran
U:s cu:cim i gi:gidahim, tanhadag u:s si ṣondadat, huḍuñigt ab ce:mo'o	Standing trees it shook, piled trash at their feet, arrived at the west
U:pam ha'ahogi i i-wuak cem ñei	Homeward it turned and looked
Jeweḍ ka:cim am ge s-keg cu'idk na:to.	The lying earth was clean and finished.
Haha ag da:m ab wu:ṣañ g tondam ce:wagi	On top of that came out the shining cloud
Da:m ka:cim baṣo mo'osc ke:k, ha'akia e-we:m ku:gc ab ke:k	To the top of the sky it bumped and stood, with many round ends it stood
At a wa i hi:.	And it went.
Jeweḍ cem si me:kotk e-elid, heg si hugid an i hi:	The earth thought it was large, but right to the edge it went
Wi:ñim cem si me:kotk e-elid, heg si hugid an i hi:	The north thought it was far, but right to the edge it went
Gamai g wakliuw si me:kotk e-elid, heg si hugid an i hi:	There the south thought it was far, but right to the edge it went

Ba'ic i ju:k cem ñei.	More it did and looked.
Ka wipiṣañ e-a:gc hekihu cem si mo:mo'imki pi a:haidam juñhim, hugid am si wui am wuihim	The small washes thought of themselves, that they would never get full, but they filled to the brim
Ba'ic i ju:k cem ñei.	More it did and looked.
Ka wopoṣañ e-a:gc cem si mo:mo'imki e-elid, heg am pi a:haidam juñhim, hugid am si wui am muihim	The large washes thought of themselves, that they would never get full, but they filled to the brim
Ge huḍuñig ab ce:mo'o.	To the west it arrived.
U:pam ha'ahogi i i-wuak cem ñei	Homeward it turned and looked
Jeweḍ ka:cim am ge s-keg wa'opagidk na:to.	The lying earth was beautifully wet and finished.
Tag da:m e-wui dahiwa g hemajkamk ha'icu a:g	On it facing each other people sat and said something
Ta am dagito ha'icu kaikam	Then they dropped some seeds
Tag da:m am wu:ṣ	Then something came out
Ha'as ṣawaḍk tatkc wu:ṣ, ha'as ṣawaḍk wa'ukc wu:ṣ, ge s-taḍañ hahakc wu:ṣ, ge s-keg muḍadagc wu:ṣ, am ge s-keg bai.	Thick root came out, thick stem came out, wide leaf came out, good tassel came out, well did it ripen
Hekaj am haha ge s-kegkam huḍuñig, s-kegkam ma:sidag.	Thus there were good evenings, good mornings.
Ha'apk hems o wa'i elidk taccua nanko ñ-i:mig.	Thus you may wish and plan, my various relatives.

We come to the fourth of Underhill's speeches, a mate from Anegam for the Santa Rosa type "B" speech. This is an unusually long and exciting text on the theme of power getting. Whereas the previous Santa Rosa speech had two *parts*, this speech has thirteen. It is one of two long texts on power getting that we will consider. The other pertains to war. Before giving the speech let us recall Brennan's words on where power getting fits into the salt pilgrimage:

After each person get through
He runs westward by the beach
As far as he wishes.

...All those that wish to
Run far west
He never looked back but
As soon as he look back
He can't go any farther,
He have to turned around
And go home.

...Many people
Are just run for miles and

Running along the shore. Drawing by Mike Chiago.

Never gets any power from the Ocean.
I suppose there are but very few
Who make their luck and become somebody
Or know something.

The Anegam speech describes one of the few.

SALT PILGRIMAGE SPEECH "B"

Jim Thomas (Dionisio), Anegam

T oi wa hab e-ju: g ñ-taccui.	Then happened what I desired.
I	I
Am huḍuñig wui g s-cuk wo:gita ka:c	Towards the west a black road lies
Kunt ag ab keiṣk i oidk gi'ik ṣoṣ	I stepped on it and followed for four stops
K ab ce:mo'o g to:wata ka:c.	Then reached where the ocean lies.
K iya eḍa hekihu ji:wia g si wo:liuwkam we:mgal	Here already had arrived the furry helper [coyote]

Ant we:gaj gi'ikho i ta'ibimhim
T kia a eḍa hekihu na:to g toha bid ñ-wa:ga.
Ka wuḍ g cukud mamcwidag hekaj an si gewṣ
Tag wui i wañckwa g wiapo'oke'el
Tag wui am daṣwa.
Ta am wua g hekaj ab i:bdaj oid si cegsat
Ta am ep wua s-i'omko ge:gyoc da:m si cegṣat
Ta am wuicudk bijim am s-o:gigko ge:gyoc da:m si cegṣat

I around him four times circled
He already had made the white clay mixture.
There was the owl wingfeather with which to tap
Towards it he pulled the grown boys
Towards it he sat them.
Then with it [feather and clay] along the heart he made a line
Then also on the right shoulder made a line
Then towards it he circled and on the left shoulder made a line

Rocky Point, the area where Papagos gathered salt.
Photo by Stanley N. Wilkes.

Wusotk hab i ju:.	Blew and did it.
Ka wuḍ komalk mo'okam hu:ñ cu'i,	There was the flat headed corn flour
Nt ag am ṣa:kud,	I took a handful
Tag am ṣa:kk am i melieu g to:wata ka:c.	Took a handful and arrived running where the ocean lies.
Ta wa cem s-ta-e:bidam e-ju:	Then so fearsomely it [ocean] did
K i hab wui si bahiwa	Towards [me] made a wave
Pi has elidk ab i miabidk ab wua g cu'i.	Not thinking [I] neared it and threw the flour.
Ab oidk i ep kioḍ	Continuing it made a wave
Pi has elidk ab i miabidk ab wua g cu'i.	Not thinking neared it and threw the flour.
Am aha wa cem s-ta-e:bidam ce'ek	Then fearsomely it sounded
Am e'eḍa betank in gei	Inside it thundered and fell
Pi has elidk ab wua g cu'i.	Not thinking [I] threw the flour.
Ab oid gi'ik kioḍ	Continuing it made four waves
Am cem s-ta-e:bidam ce'ek	There fearsomely it sounded
Am e'eḍa betank ab da:m i'ikioḍ	Inside it thundered and on top it rolled
Am we:gaj geik ab aha wa ke:k c ab eḍa ha'icu cem ñeid.	Behind it [I] fell and stood and inside it looked at something.
II	II
Am aha wa u:pam i wu:ṣañ	Then came back out
Am aha wa hugid an i me:	Then along the [ocean] side ran
K am hebai ai si wo:liuwkam we:mgal, mehedam wu:pkam t-we:mgal	Someplace reached the furry helper, our burning eyed helper [coyote]
K cem s-ta-e:bidam e-wuak ab wui si me:	Very fearsomely he acted but towards him [I] ran
Pi has elidk i miabidk ab wua g cu'i.	Not thinking threw the flour.
Tk am hab i me:, tk am i me:, tk am i me:, am amjeḍ am bṣ i hi:	Then he [coyote] ran, and he ran, and he ran, and then just walked
Ta am i oidk am ep ai	Continued and [I] reached him again
T am ab sikoli ṣi meḍk am we:gaj i da'ibij	He made a fast circle and went around behind
Pi has elidk i miabidk ab wua g cu'i.	Not thinking [I] neared him and threw the flour.
Gam hab si hi:, am oidk am ai	Away he walked, continuing [I] reached him
Am aha wa ab si toḍk i siwotka ab si s-ge:sim e-wua	Then he barked and crouched down and got ready to bite
An aha wa ke:kiwak am a:gid	Then he stopped and said
"Aheu'u cu:cuḍ mapt hemu iñ-wo:po'ik b i hemapa g ñ-cu'ijig	"Yes nephew, so now you will get it away from me and gather up my doings
Hebai wa:mdag s-ñeidam ma:culig."	Someplace farther ahead is an interesting teaching."
Am aha wa i beik am aha wa bei, ñ-ab hugid an ke:kiwa	Then he grabbed [me], then grabbed [me], I stood next to him
Ge ka:cim ab hugid añ bei.	Beside the ocean he took [me].

III

Ku:bs wepogi heg weco i bebbehi

Gahi am wu:ṣad
Am hebai ai g ṣu:dagi s-hadam
Heg wui am u'apa
"Do:wai, cu:cuḍ, map wuḍ o si cioj, wo we:s i:k o ñ-wo:po'ik b i hemapa g ñ-cu'ijig."
Ta am keiṣk am i'ik si hu g wi'idajc i dagiumc si kawoḍkadk bei.

III

Smoke likeness [spray] below he took [me]
On the other side came out
Someplace reached the sticky water
Towards that he brought [me]
"Now, nephew, if you are a real man, you will drink it all and get it away from me and gather up all my doings."
Then [I] stepped and drank and finished the remainders and scraped it and gathered it and took it.

IV

Ba'ic i bei
Am hebai ai g ṣu:dagi mamtod
K am u'apa
"Do:wai, cu:cuḍ, p wuḍ o si cioj, wo we:s i:k o ñ-wo:po'i b i hemapa g ñ-cu'ijig"
Ta am keiṣ am i'ik si hu, wi'idaj si kawoḍkadk bei.

IV

Again took [me]
Someplace reached the mossy water
There brought [me]
"Now, nephew, if you are a real man, you will drink it all and get it away from me and gather all my doings"
Then [I] stepped and drank and finished it, the remainders gathered and took.

V

Am ba'ic i bei
Am hebai ai g s-u'am ṣu:dagi
K am u'apa
"Do:wai, cu:cuḍ, p wuḍ o si cioj, wo we:s i:k o ñ-wo:po'i b i hemapa g ñ-cu'ijig"
Ta am keiṣk am i'ik si hu, wi'idaj si kawoḍkadk bei.

V

Again took [me]
Someplace reached the yellow water
There brought [me]
"Now, nephew, if you are a real man, you will drink it all and get it away from me and gather all my doings"
Then stepped and drank and finished it, the remainders gathered and took.

VI

Am ba'ic i bei
Am hebai ai g e'edam ṣu:dagi
K am u'apa
"Do:wai, cu:cuḍ, p wuḍ o si cioj, wo we:s i:k o ñ-wo:po'i b i hemapa g ñ-cu'ijig"
Ta am keiṣk am i'ik si hu, wi'idaj si kawoḍkadk bei.
Am ep ke:kiwak am a:gid
"Mapt hemu i ñ-wo:po'i, hemapa ñ-cu'ijig
Hebai wa:mdag s-ñeidam ma:culig."

VI

Again took [me]
Someplace reached the bloody water
There brought [me]
"Now, nephew, if you are a real man, you will drink it all and get it away from me and gather all my doings"
Then stepped and drank and finished it, the remainders gathered and took.
Again he stood and said
"Then now get it away from me, gather my doings
Someplace farther ahead is an interesting teaching."

VII

Am hab i bebbehim
Am ahi g jeweḍaj.
Taṣ huḍuñig baṣo ke:k g siw hewel

Pi ba:bagi ta-ji:wim cu'ig, an we:gaj g jeweḍ si wi'umsc ka:c
Pi ba:bagi ta-ji:wim cu'ig, g wui ab u'apa
Da:m i dadahim, am ul g e-nowi
Ab bei, ab si ba:bagi i no:l
E'ed ka'akwuḍ i wo:p
Eḍa ab bei g hogi sikol
U:s ṣopol, ga:t gi'adam, ṣel da'adam wapk cu'idam, s-cu-cu'akanadkam wainom
K heg ab we:nadc a u:pam i noḍagid.

VII

Then he was taking [me]
Then reached his land.
At the base of the sunset stands the bitter wind
Not slowly to be approached it is, around it the land very flooded lies
Not slowly to be approached it is, towards it he took [me]
On it jumping, he reached out his arm
Took it, slowly bent down
Blood in balls was running
Then took the leather shield
Short stick, bowstring, straight flying clean reed, good for stabbing iron

Those put together and turned towards home.

VIII

K an ai g ṣu:dagi, g eḍa g ma:kai am daha
Heg wui am ke:ṣwak am a:gid
"Mapt am has o ju: m do:da g ñ-cu:cuḍ i ant u'apa?"
Am o i wu:ṣañ g s-to:ta ciaka, ab to'i.

VIII

Reached the water, a medicine man there sat
Towards him he stepped and said
"What are you going to do to my nephew that I brought here?"
Took out his white power and put it on [me].

IX

K an ai g ṣu:dagi mamtoḍ, g eḍa g ma:kai am daha
Heg wui am ke:ṣwak am a:gid
"Mapt am has o ju: m do:da g ñ-cu:cuḍ i ant u'apa?"
Am o i wu:ṣañ g s-cehedagi ciaka ab to'i.

IX

Then reached the mossy water, a medicine man there sat
Towards him stepped and said
"What are you going to do to my nephew that I brought here?"
He took out his green power and put it on [me].

X

K'an ai g s-u'am ṣu:dagi, g eḍa g ma:kai am daha
Heg wui am ke:ṣwak am a:gid
"Mapt am has o ju: m do:da g ñ-cu:cuḍ i ant u'apa?"
Am i wu:ṣañ g s-u'am ciaka, ab to'i.

X

Then reached the yellow water a medicine man there sat
Towards him stepped and said
"What are you going to do to my nephew that I brought here?"
He took out his yellow power and put it on.

XI

K an ai g e'edam ṣu:dagi, g eḍa g ma:kai am daha
Heg wui am ke:ṣwak am a:gid
"Mapt am has o ju: m do:da g ñ-cu:cuḍ i ant u'apa?"
Am i wu:ṣañ g s-wegi ciaka, ab to'i.

XI

Then reached the bloody water, a medicine man there sat
Towards him stepped and said
"What are you going to do to my nephew that I brought here?"
He took out his red power and put it on.

XII

K ab u:pam i bei
Am ep ai g to:wata ka:cim
Am ep hugid an bei g ku:bs wepogi k weco am i bei
Gahi am ep wu:ṣad am i beik am melkuḍ eḍa dagito.

Kut ab aha wa keiṣk i oi
Si'alig ce:mo'ok gahu mel.

Eḍa ab mu:gia g u'adam

Pi ha koṣc ñeid.
Ṣel himadc ab no:nhait ab eḍa dagṣ

In hu si s-winam ju:, am ñeid.

XII

Homeward took [me]
Again arrived where the ocean lies
Again to the side took the smoke likeness [spray] and under it took [me]
Again crossed through it and took [me] and at the running place dropped [me].
Then [I] stepped on it and continued
Reached the east and arrived there running.
There sat bent over the bringer [of the salt getters]
Not sleeping and watching.
[I] Walked straight and pressed on his hands
In there tightly put it, then looked.

XIII

Ab i wu:ṣ g yo:ṣ t-ma:m
Tag eḍa ab i ñeidc ab i oi g wo:g
Gi'ik ab ṣoṣk ia ai g jeweḍga

Ta am e-wo'ikud weco hiṣpk wo'iṣk wo'iwa.
Koi he'es o kut am s-keg s-ha'icuk na:to g wiapo'oke'el
S-keg naumki ñe'i, s-keg sikolim ñe'i, s-keg wuaga hekaj g cu:wa'am pi a eḍacud
S-ki:mkam wiapoi heg am ma:ck am pi hiwgid, hekaj g huḍuñig am ṣaṣawk

Am e-ce: g si'alig ke:k, hekaj s-ap kaidam wu:ṣañ do:da'ag cu:cim
Hekaj ṣaṣawk cu:cwa g u:s ke:kam
Hekaj si tatk ke:kiwa.

XIII

Then came out the sun
Then [I] looked and followed the road
Took four starts and here reached [my] land
Then under the bed buried it and lay down.
Soon after the young man makes something good
Good drunkeness songs, good circling songs, good young girl songs with which to bother the young girl
The homeloving young boy will know and won't permit it, therefore the evening will echo
Dawn comes, therefore nice sounds come from the standing mountains
Therefore echoing stand the trees
Therefore well rooted they stand.

There is one more speech to give but we must first put order into what we have. The most noteworthy fact about the salt pilgrimage speeches given so far is that they fall into two types. In oratory and in actual timing, the pilgrimage forms a transition from the wine feast. One would be hard pressed on first view to distinguish a type "A" salt pilgrimage speech from a wine feast speech. The only surface difference that separates them is that the latter always mention wine, no matter how briefly and obliquely, and the salt pilgrimage speeches never do.

Let us propose, contrary to Underhill's earlier statements, that the type "A" salt pilgrimage speech always precedes the type "B" and that the type "A" speech is given early in the journey while the type "B" is given on the eve of arriving at the ocean. This is the pattern of Anegam and Wainom Ke:k; let us suppose it was the pattern of Santa Rosa, too. We can then trace developments from "A" to "B" in the same manner as was done with the sequence of wine feast speeches; we can look for a larger order than that which is contained in one speech.

As we have seen, the "A" speeches are always eastward. They involve an eastward journey to a rainhouse, the use of tobacco, and a petition to a 'made father' for rain. The "B" speeches in contrast are westward. The short Santa Rosa type "B" speech does not mention the ocean. It includes the use of tobacco smoke to gain the 'made father's' attention, analogous to the rainhouse speeches. The long Anegam speech describes a plunge into the ocean with no preliminary use of tobacco. The hero follows a 'black road' in contrast to the 'shining' or 'white' roads previously associated with tobacco smoke. When he reaches the 'made fathers', beginning with Coyote, the hero deals with them in an intimate manner, in contrast to the petitioning behavior of the heroes of the other speeches. He obtains power from them. There is a clear opposition between an eastern rainhouse, a white road (tobacco smoke), and rain; and the western ocean, a black road (no smoking mentioned), and power. The Santa Rosa type "B" speech is in between with a westward road (no color mentioned), an indistinct place (no ocean or rainhouse mentioned), tobacco smoke, and power. It is therefore the Anegam "B" speech that interests us: Does it represent a development from the type "A" speeches analogous to the development from the 'running' to the 'seating' speeches of the wine feast?

The key to the development in the salt pilgrimage speeches is that the hero does not drink at the place of the rainhouse-dwelling 'made father' in the type "A" speeches, but he does drink at the place of the ocean-dwelling 'made father'. He drinks all of Coyote's various waters. This aligns the two sets of speeches. It is recalled that no drinking was done at the rainhouse visited in the 'running' speech, either. The hero's visit was to invite the inhabitant of the house (we must not call him a 'made father' because that term is not used in the wine feast oratory) to attend a feast at the hero's village. In the wine feast sequence, the guest-host dialogue is carried into the second 'seating' speech: The inviter serves wine to his rain god guest. A switch occurs in the type "B" salt pilgrimage speech. There is no more talk of rainhouses. The action now takes place at the ocean. The human hero drinks of his 'made father's' liquids. The result is not rain, but power. On the level of the *dramatis personnae* the switch is that the human hero is now the guest, the 'made father' is now the host. It is as if the human hero attends a god's wine feast.

While it may be pure coincidence, we must note that in both expressions of drinking, the guest comes from the east. Thus, the host village at a wine feast always occupies the western position on its ceremonial ground and the wine is always carried from a 'round house' in that direction. The events at the ocean in the Anegam type "B" speech reiterate that relationship. Guest is east and host is west.

We come now to the final salt pilgrimage speech which represents the phase of celebration and purification after the pilgrims' return. We will compare it to the mockingbird speech which terminates the oratory at the wine feast. It has elements of that speech, but elements as well of the type "A" salt pilgrimage speech: It tells of a visit to a 'made father' at a rainhouse, this time in the west.

Underhill was not sure if this was the proper speech for closing the pilgrimage: "No one was found who knew the (proper) Santa Rosa speech. The one recited is a variation of the material used in the previous speech, The Marking (i.e., our type "A"—1946:327)." It is from Jose Moreno of Santa Rosa. No Anegam version was collected, so we cannot discuss that village's sequel to its stirring type "B" speech.

Before giving the speech let us sketch the events of the purification. They take place at night on the ceremonial ground east of the round house. Salt and other tokens brought back from the ocean (shells, etc.) are placed in the middle of the ground near a fire. The salt getters sit on the north, the men who sing for them sit on the south. Spectators sit to the east. According to Underhill, medicine men sat at the west "to perceive any sickness or evil which might be present (1946:241)." It is not recorded whether they ministered over the salt getter or the salt.

Both Brennan and Underhill state that the singers pressed their scraping stick musical instruments onto the salt getters after singing their songs. In addition Underhill learned that the singers breathed "power" upon the salt getters, which the latter inhaled; and that at dawn bits of purified salt were given to everyone present to inhale (1946:241).

We may relate the above to the 'sit and drink' as follows: Salt (from the west), the singers' musical instruments (placed to the south on the ritual ground), and the singers' breath replace wine as the substances that are transmitted from hosts to guests. The placement of individuals in the guest role to the north (the returned salt getters) as well as the east (the spectators) requires comment, as does the placement of hosts to the south (the singers) as well as the west (the medicine men). Very simply, south is an alternative or secondary direction of the ocean. Papagos use two words for the south, *wakliw tagio* 'driftwood direction' and *ka:cim tagio*, 'lying (water) direction'. The first term refers to the 'downhill' direction in which water carries driftwood after a rain, and 'downhill' essentially means 'towards the ocean'. The second word refers to the ocean itself. Thus, while the salt speeches systematically locate the ocean to the west *(huḍuñig tagio*, 'descent direction', in reference to the sunset), the vocabulary of directions places it to the south. In geographical fact both are correct. We may conclude from this that there is nothing wrong, either in geography or in logic, with an ocean ritual that divides its guests and hosts as this rite does. More interesting is the question of why the speeches assign the ocean to a direction that runs counter to the vocabulary—to 'sunset direction' rather than 'lying direction'. They do so because it is geographically permissable, but also, it is suggested, for the sake of opposition with the predominate direction of the summer rains.

We turn now to the text of the type "C" speech. No Papago transcription is available for it. We give Underhill's translation below, exactly as it appeared in *Papago Indian Religion* (1946:237-38).

SALT PELGRIMAGE SPEECH"C"

Jose Moreno, Santa Rosa

The remains of the cigarette did I place
upright [in the fire, to light it].
I put it to my lips,
I smoked.

To the rain house standing in the west I
came.
All kinds of mist were bound up there,
And I could not [unbind them].
It was my cigarette smoke.
Circling around it, it entered and
unbound them.
I tried to see him, my guardian,
But squarely turned away from me
he sat.
It was my cigarette smoke.
Circling around, it turned him toward
me.

Thus I spoke, to him, my guardian.
"What will happen?
Most wretched lies the earth which you
have made.
The trees which you have planted,
leafless stand.
The birds you threw in the air,
They perch and do not sing.
The springs of water are gone dry.
The beasts which run upon the earth,
They make no sound."
Thus I said.
"What will befall the earth which you
have made?"
Then, thus spake he, my guardian.
"Is this so difficult?
You need but gather and recite the
ritual.
Then, knowing all is well,
Go to your homes."

Then back I turned.
Eastward, I saw, the land was sloping
laid.
Slowly along I went.
I reached my former sleeping place and
laid me down.
Thus, four days did I travel toward the
east.
Then in the west a wind arose,
Well knowing whither it should blow.
Up rose a mist and towered toward the
sky,
And others stood with it, their tendrils
touching.
Then they moved.
Although the earth seemed very wide,
Clear to the edge of it did they go.
Although the north seemed very far,
Clear to the edge of it did they go.
Although the south seemed very far,
Clear to the edge of it did they go.
Then to the east they went, and looking
back,
They saw the earth lie beautifully moist
and finished.

Then out flew Blue Jay shaman;
Soft feathers he pulled out and let them
fall.
The earth was blue [with flowers].

Then out flew Yellow Finch shaman;
Soft feathers he pulled out and let them
 fall,
Till the earth was yellow [with flowers].
Thus it was fair, our year.
Thus should you also think,
All you my kinsmen.

Like the mockingbird speech, this one ends with a rain that involves birds (blue and yellow ones, not mockingbirds). The reference is to a very gentle form of rain that falls in Papago country in the late winter. In contrast to the summer rains, this form comes predominantly from the west. It is the same kind of rain as was described in the westward mockingbird speech. Both texts state that the rains crossed the earth and wetted it. Similar crossings are found in the other mockingbird speeches and in the type "A" salt pilgrimage speeches, but the rain from the west is described in much gentler terms. Missing is the spectacular and ecstatic language appropriate to thunderstorms.

The gentleness of the rains carries over into the "C" speech's reference to birds. These must be seen as counterparts to the mockingbirds. Their function in the "C" speech is to drop feathers which become flowers. Spring is the wild flower season in the desert and, as we noted, the rains that bring them are from the west. Thus, the speech refers to a well defined phenomenon. As part of a summer ritual, however, the speech anticipates the season of reference.

The wild flowers are counterparts to the wild greens, grasses, and cactuses of the westward mockingbird speech. Whenever a western rainhouse is referred to, the vegetation that results from its moisture is wild as opposed to cultivated plants (we will have another instance of this in the chapter on flood). The question is why the mockingbird speech fixed on wild food plants and the "C" speech fixed on wild flowers. It is recalled that the type "A" speeches, which treat of an eastern rainhouse, run the gamut of types of vegetation. Brennan's speech has wild foods (grass, trees, and saguaro cactus) just as the westward mockingbird speech. The Santa Rosa "A" speech has farm crops just as the east, south, and north mockingbird speeches. The Anegam "A" speech is noncommittal on this issue, saying that the earth became 'spongy' but not saying what grew.

The array may be understood as having two fixed points with a transitional zone in between (Table 5). One fixed point is the association of farm crops with an

TABLE 5

RAINHOUSES AND VEGETATION

	Eastern Rainhouse:	*Western Rainhouse:*
Farm Crops:	Mockingbird speech Santa Rosa "A" speech	
Wild Crops	Brennan "A" speech	Mockingbird speech
Wild Flowers:		Santa Rosa "C" speech

eastern rainhouse, the other is the association of wild flowers with a rainhouse in the west. As was indicated above, two actual types and seasons of rain are involved, summer thunderstorms from the east, and light winter showers from the west. It is suggested that the wine feast concentrates on the former type, but includes reference to a western rainhouse "for completeness;" and the salt pilgrimage, oriented to the west, concentrates on the latter type. The salt pilgrimage oratory gets to its proper rain in the "C" speech, after a transition through the type "A" speeches.

Finally, how do power and the ocean pertain to the "C" speech? They do not pertain. We cannot improve on Underhill's earlier perception of the "C" speech as a variation of the "A" speech in regard to power and the ocean. Let us elaborate on it, however. It is recalled that there is no rainhouse in the "B" speeches. The scene has shifted, in the Anegam speech at least, to the ocean itself which represents a different configuration from any rainhouse. The ocean is a limitless expanse of salt water while a rainhouse is an enclosed concentration of clouds that produce fresh water. The west has both kinds of places, a winter drizzle producing rainhouse and an ocean. The other directions have a complementary and economically more important form of rainhouse, but, as far as the speeches are concerned, they lack oceans. Of these other directions the eastern rainhouse is primary, being the first mentioned in the wine feast orations, and the only rainhouse mentioned in the type "A" salt pilgrimage speeches. Such is the evidence from the texts; we will take up the experiential basis of these ideas in the final chapter.

Now the Anegam "B" speech mentions no rainhouse, but it has power granting 'made fathers' at the ocean. How do these 'made fathers' differ from the inhabitants of rainhouses? The hero's experience with these 'made fathers' began as soon as he reached the ocean. He met Coyote there and was marked by him with white clay. The hero plunged repeatedly into the ocean. When he came out the final time he had the following adventures: First he drank various of Coyote's 'waters' (parts III-VI); then he went to Coyote's 'land' where the 'bitter wind' also resides (part VIII); then he journeyed to yet another series of waters which were presided over by 'medicine men' (parts VIII-XI). The language of 'made father' and 'nephew' is used throughout indicating that this series of 'made father' encounters had the purpose of making the hero into a medicine man—quite a different purpose from the encounters at any rainhouse.

Those other encounters typically have the hero travel on a 'road' formed of tobacco smoke to reach his destination. The analogue to this road in the type "B" speech is the hero's passage through the ocean. What is the difference? The journeys to rainhouses sound as if they were made on dry land. The hero walked. He was followed by his winds and clouds as in the 'running' and 'return' speeches. He could breathe. An ocean plunge is a more drastic form of journey, a passage through the transparent, liquid, airless, medium of salt water. We must understand that earth is one element, air is another, and water is still another. People drown in water; they must swim, float, or "fly" through it, but may not walk on it.

Once the hero had passed through the ocean, he drank and was ministered to in various other ways: he was given things to bundle and take home, objects were pressed on his body, etc. There is more bodily activity in the type "B" speech than in a rainhouse speech. The following is the typical rainhouse scenario: The hero arrives, he uses smoke to turn the owner towards him, the two talk, and the owner consents to send his breath and clouds to water the earth. The word 'touch' *(ta:t)* is used in the 'running' and 'return' speeches. A donation of seeds is mentioned, in the Anegam type "A" speech, but these are exceptions that prove the rule: rain gods are aloof while in their rainhouses.

Thus there appear to be two ideal types of god: rainhouse dwellers, of whom the eastern is primary, and power givers, who so far are associated only with the west. The point of the wine feast is to invite the first type of god to come to humanity and drink, the point of the salt pilgrimage is to be invited to drink by the second type of god in the god's own territory.

Rabbit hunt. Drawing by Mike Chiago.

Hunting

This chapter concerns three different rites which revolve around hunting and connect that activity with rain, dryness, farming, and sickness. The most important of the rites, called *ma'm'aga*, will be interpreted as a closing of the rainy season that includes the wine feast and salt pilgrimage. It comes in 'Dry grass moon', around the fall equinox, at the time of the harvest. Its purpose is to make fresh farm crops safe for eating. The danger that they pose is diarrhoea, an an affliction that is linked to wine drinking and to the ocean. We will proceed from a pure and simple hunting rite, which is for small game, to the deer hunt of the *ma'm'aga*, and then to a cleansing ritual called *a'ada* which sometimes accompanies and is sometimes separated from the *ma'm'aga*.

RABBIT HUNT SPEECH

Bernabe Lopez, San Pedro

At a hemu p e-ju: g ñ-taccuidag na:nko ñ-i:mig.	Now has happened what I wished, my various relatives.
Kunt am u:g ñ-bei, nt a cem ñei	I raised myself, I looked
Tag taṣ abṣ cem sikol me:	The sun in a circle ran
Kunt a hab e-ju: g ñ-taccuidag	And so it happened what I wished
Kunt ab i wanckwa g wiapo'ol ke'el.	I pulled out the grown boys.
I	I
Kunt a hab a:gk na:to	I had a purpose and did it
Am ñ-bebbehim, ab ñ-wo'i u:s ṣont ab.	There I took myself, there laid myself at a tree base.
Tag wui am ku:g g hab ñ-elidag	There my wishes stopped
Kunt ag wui wo'ogculid.	Towards that I made a road.
Kunt ag oid am i wanmeḍ g ñ-wiapo'o ke'elga	Along that I led my grown boys
Nt a ab i mia g ki:c eḍ da:kam, al na:kc oimmeḍdam,gewpk wopokam.	I neared the house-in sitter [ground squirrel], the earred runner [rabbit], the stiff haired one [rat]
Kut ag taṣ abṣ gamai cem ju:pi.	Then the sun had nearly set.

II	II
Nt a u'apa g ñ-mu'a	I brought my kill
K eḍa am wu:ṣ g keli o'odham	Then came out the old man
Kut elko, am si gewiomi.	He skinned it and pounded.
Kut am wu:ṣ g oks	Then came out the old lady
Am ha-ui g waikk ma:makai, at a am da:ṣ.	She took the three medicine men [stones], set them.
Kut ag eḍa ha-cu:cwa g honowitaj.	Within in them they stood the huggers [firewood]
At a am bei g ha'a, am tai.	Then they took the pot, then lit a fire.
Kut abṣ cem huḍ g taṣ	And the sun set
Kut a gamai bia, tag am gamai hu ge agṣpi ka'kel.	Then they served it, away hanging they carried it.
Kuñ a ge'e s-ap'e ñ-taccuidagk elid	That was my good wish and thought
Kumpt ha'ap o elidk o taccua, na:nko ñ-i:mig.	You could think thus and wish, my various relatives.

It was common practice in the 1930s and before to hold a communal rabbit hunt at the time of the wine feast. No rule said that one had to be held then. There could be wine feasts without rabbit hunts and vice versa. The reason for combining the two was perhaps practical. The summer rains had started and the rabbits were, as Underhill was told, "fat and lazy." Many people had assembled for the coming festivities so there was ample manpower. The hunt was for men and boys only. Moreover, in old times the success of the hunt most probably determined how long the wine celebration could last. The rabbits and other small game would provide food for the drinkers.

When combined with the wine feast, the hunt took place on the day between the first and second night of singing. It will be recalled that this was an "empty" day in the wine feast program. When filled out, there would be a night of dancing, a day of hunting, a second night of dancing, and then the 'sit and drink'. It is interesting that the songs and oratory of the wine feast make no reference to a rabbit hunt. Neither, as we have seen, does the oratory of the hunt make reference to a wine feast. The two events could perfectly well be done independently of each other.

Because the hunt was typically sandwiched between nights belonging to another rite, its own ritualism was cut to the minimum. In terms of our general scheme, only the third phase, the hunt itself, was ritualized; and this phase was confined to the daylight hours of one day. In terms of time and "completeness" of ritualization, the rabbit hunt is the shortest and simplest of the ceremonies described in this book.

Its program was as follows: Sometime prior to the hunt a brush fence was erected a short distance from the village. This was done without ceremony. Perhaps the same fence was used year after year. On the appointed day, for example, on the morning after the first night of rain dancing, the men and boys of a village, plus their 'hunt chief', arrived at the fence. Once they were there, the hunt chief made a speech such as the one given above. After the speech, the hunt chief and some good marksmen stationed themselves by a gap that had been left in the middle of the fence line. The rest of the party divided into halves, each half going to an end of the fence. They formed two curving lines like pincers and gradually drove the game to the marksmen waiting at the hole in the fence.

The speech is quite regular in structure with a short preface, a two part body, and a short conclusion. It is a down to earth description of a hunt, an oration about what the participants in the rite were actually doing. It was the only bit of ritual speech used in the hunt—there were no songs or special "symbolic" acts so far as is known.

DEER HUNT

Underhill collected information on the deer hunts of four villages: Santa Rosa, Kaka, Pisinimo, and Quitovac (Sonora). These represent four different dialect groups and four distinct historical traditions. The breadth of coverage for this rite is greater than for any of the other rites considered in this book.

We will start with the Santa Rosa rite because it is the only one of the four that regularly included an *a'ada*. At Santa Rosa the preparations began with an oration. This was not recorded because the rite was in disuse by the time of Underhill's visit in the 1930s—but we have one from Kaka, below. The second phase, the journey out, was set for a number of days after the opening oration.

The journey out apparently took just one day—it was a question of meeting at mountains a short distance from the village. Underhill does not mention any ceremonies during the night before the hunt, but these existed as the following narrative by Juan Gregorio of Santa Rosa makes clear. The nighttime ceremonies were similar to those of a wine feast. Songs were sung while medicine men who accompanied the party used their powers to determine the location of the object sought (clouds or deer). Apparently there was no oratory during this phase, only singing.

THE *MA'M'AGA*

Juan Gregorio, Santa Rosa

Hab o o-ju:	It will happen
Am o wa ke:k g ahidag	The [time of the] year will stand
Matp has i masma hebai hab o e-ju:	When somehow they [people] will do,
Ko s-kegad ha'icu	And will fix something [crops]
Mañ im hu hab a:.	As I have said.
Ab ahawa bṣ o ol i i-na:tohimk	But they will just be getting ready
Mas o o-hu:	That they could be eaten
Mo hab hia e-wuad	As of course is done
S-waḍag e-kua ha'icu.	[in the] wet [fresh] eating of something.
Hu:ñ, mu:ñ, ha:l ma:maḍ, mi:lon	Corn, beans, baby squash, mellon
M am he'kia ha'icu ab wu:ṣañ ab jeweḍ.	Of the many things that come out of the earth.

Pegi kc aṣ hab a cu'ig
Matp hems ab ka:c g mumkidag.
Pegi k g hab a:gc hab wua hegai
Mat gm hu o i kegc
Kut gm hu i da:m o o-hug
K gm hu abṣ o s-ap'ek.

Well but it will be the case
That a sickness may lay [on them].
Well and that is why they do that one,
That they will fix it [crops]
Then later on it can be eaten
Later on it will be all right.

Ñe: i:da, hekid o i taccud g je:ñim o'odham
Mat hab o o-ju:
K am o i ha-ui g t-wipiopga
Mat o hihim ko ga: g huawi.
Ñe:k woho mo hab e-wuad
T am o hihim
K hebai wo i huḍuñig wua
Matp hebai hasko i hihi.
K im hab hia si hihhim gammai hab
Mo hab hema g al gahi jeg g do'ag.

Look, this [man], when the smoker [headman] man wants it
That they will do it [ceremony]
And they will get our boys
That they will go and hunt the deer.
Look, and it's true that it happens
They will go
And someplace it will be sunset
Wherever they have gone off to.
And they will be going along there
Where there is an opening in the mountain.

Ab atp hebai hasko hia
Pi itp hab hu hia si ab
In atp hu abṣ hebai
Mat ab huḍuñig wua.
Ñe: k cuhug
Mat am o ñe'icul
K hab wuḍ a'aga ṣ wuḍ ku:ṣada ñe'i hegai.

It's just off someplace,
It's not right against it [mountain]
It's just off someplace
Where it is sunset.
Look and it's dark
Then they will sing for it
And it is called *ku:sada* songs.

Pegi, t am eḍa am wo a ep ha-u'ad g ha'icu ñeidam
Mo cuckagad am o e-mamce ha'icu.

Well and for that they will also have brought some seers
Who in the darkness will figure out something.

Am o ho-daḍṣ
T in hi wa ñe'ed hegam.
Kutp hegam am o daḍhak
C am hasko ob hi o wu:pad e-cegitoidag.
Ñe: k oi a hebai hab e-wua a woho
Matp am o hema tagio
T hekid am o i ku:gt
—Pi itp hi wa ma:si
Matp he'es hab o i ce'ek

They will seat them
Then of course they will sing.
And those [medicine men] will be sitting
And someplace will throw their thoughts.
Look and sometimes it truly happens
That it is in the direction of one of them
So when it [singing] finishes
—It may not be dawn yet
But they [singers] will have sounded enough

Mo i ku:gt
—Am hu i s-ap'ek a'aga
Matp am o a heki hu ha'icu i s-mai hegam
Mo heg amjeḍ ha-u'a.

So they are finished
—Maybe it is all right and it means
That they have already found something out
Those who were brought for that reason.

Ñe: k woho	Look and it's true
Mat am hab o cei g e-ñeida	That one will speak his seeings
Matp has i masma ha'icu am ta:tk am heg i oidam.	How he felt something during it [the singing].
Am hebai ha'ap o a:	In some direction he will tell
Mat ha'ap o—.	So in that direction they will—[go to hunt the deer].
Kutp hema hab o cu'igkad am we:hejed	And to one of them [medicine men] it may be the case
Mat im hu go'olko ep hi o a. hegai.	That he may tell to go off in another direction.
Pegi t am ha'ap ha'i o hihi	Well, and that way some of them will go
O hems hab o cei am o abṣ i we:s hab ma:s hegai	Or perhaps he [medicine man] will say that they [deer] all showed up
Mat a ha'ap o ga: hegai.	So in that direction they will [all] search.
Ñe: k a woho o ma:s, s-cuhugam.	Look and it's true that it's like that in the night.
K atp o ñene	Then they will awaken [after resting]
K am hascu o ol i na:to	And a little something they will make
Matp hascu i cuiṣcuk.	That will be their lunch.
O ki aṣ al s-e:keg	Yet it's still dim
Koi at o i si ma:si	It hasn't yet really gotten dawn
—T o hihi.	—They will go.

The day of hunting was not like a usual hunt because the deer was killed without shedding its blood. It was caught and strangled, Underhill was told. There was a short ceremony prior to returning home. A speech was given and the deer was butchered for transport back to the village. Again we have no Santa Rosa version of this speech, but will give one below from Kaka.

The journey home, phase four, was without ritual. It was made in the afternoon of the day of the hunt. On Underhill's information nothing was done in the night following the hunt. The celebration of the return began the next day. The meat was cooked without salt by old women. Meanwhile the men cleansed every house in the village. This is the *a'ada*, the discussion of which we delay until later. Suffice it to say that it involves collecting sickness with thorny cholla cactus branches.

Full *a'ada*'s were not always done but something related to them was a standard feature. Fresh green crops of corn, squash and mellon were brought to the site of the cooking. Each family brought a token from its fields. The crops and the meat were cleaned with the same thorny branches that were used for the houses throughout the village.

Following the various cleanings, in the late afternoon or night, there was singing and dancing. The dancers were two boys and two girls, the boys with arrows over their right shoulders, the girls with an ear of corn in each hand (Underhill, 1946:109). During the dancing or after it, the cooked meat and crops were given to the assembled people to eat.

Let us return to Juan Gregorio's account of the cleaning of the crops as it was practiced in Santa Rosa:

Ñe:, heg hekid am o i we:s e-hemapa hegai	Look, when they will have gathered all of it
Mañ hab ep a:g, ha'icu wu:ṣdag	As I have said, the crops
Mat ab al i e-na:to	Which are just getting ready
Am heki hu ep o o-ui mu'i ha'icu	They will have brought many things [to the dance ground]
Am o o-tua amai	They will put them there
Pegi, t hegam mo om wuḍ ha'icu ñeidam	Well, and those who are seers
Ma:makai b am ha-a'aga	Medicine men you call them
Wo wi:piñhu we:s hegai	They will suck all that
Mo he'ekia ha'icu am i we:c.	As many things [crops] as lay there.
Ñe:, am hekid o i ku:gt	Look, when they finish
Gm hu hebai i ju: g taṣ	When the sun sets
Pegi, tp am aha wo ui g je:ñim o'odham	Well, the headman will take it [sucked out sickness]
K am o i u'ugk atp hebai o i hiaṣ.	He will take it up and then bury it someplace.
Aṣ am hab juppid hegai ha'icu has s-ta:hadkam mumkidag	The bad feeling sickness will just sink
Matp ab hu hab o cu'ig abai	Whatever was there [in the crops]
Matp am o o-wi:piñhuñ amai	That was sucked out
Ñe:, im hu o i e-paḍc hegai	Look, and it [sickness] will be ruined
Pegi, t am hekid o i s-ap s-ta-hugima	Well, and whenever it is properly ready to eat
To hu:	They'll eat it
Gamai hu abṣ o ge s-ap'ek.	By that time it will be all right.
Hebai o hab e-wuadc hab masma hab e-a'aga	Sometimes it happens that way, they say
Maṣ wakwidag b o hia a'aga hegai	That it is diarrhoea as they say
Mat hab masma o ho-memelic	Which makes them run
Mat pi o e-kegcudask hegai.	If they don't properly clean it [fresh crops].

We see that the medicine man sucks sickness from the new crops, otherwise people would get diarrhoea from them. It is important to understand that these are fresh crops, still green. The *ma'm'aga* with its deer hunting is meant to make them fit to eat, as if they would be inedible by people in their natural state. Mr. Gregorio was clear on this as he continued his discussion. He explained that, as a substitute for a complete *ma'm'aga*, people would sometimes simply bring a green squash or mellon for a medicine man to treat at his house. They would then take the treated objects back to the field and leave them there so that their cleanness would spread to the rest of the crops.

Ñe:, k eḍa ab himdam hab ep e-wua e:p	Look, later it was done like this, too
Mo hemu pi im hu hab e-wua	Since now they never do it [*ma'm'aga*]
Kutp heg eñigakam an e-oid eḍ an o ñei	So the owner will see something in his field
Mat has masma hab o o-ju:	How it [crop] is doing [ripening]
Kut an o ha'icu al i bei	And he will take a little something
Ha:l, mi:loñ, hu:ñ mam he'ekia ha'icu wuḍ o ik	Squash, mellon, corn, as many things as there may be
Pegi, k am o u'apa heg wui hegai	Well, and he will bring it to him [medicine man]
Mo heḍai wuḍ i mat hab o ju:	Whoever will be the one to do it
Pegi, t am o i kegcunad.	Well, and he will clean it.
Ṣa ba hab hia mat gd hu o u:hum o woi	But then he must put it back again
Matp hebai i bei anai	From where he got it
Gḍ hu si s-eḍawk o woi	There in the center [of the field] he will lay it
T im hu a'ai hab o cu'ig	Then it will go in all ways
T o wa hi: g gewkdaj	The strength will go
K o wa al ce:mo'o	It will permeate it [field]
K we:s o ma'iṣ hegai gawul ma:s ha'icu	It will cover all the different kinds of things [new crops]
Matp hebai o i cu:ck	Where they stand
Pegi, t am hab o wa ep ju:, ha'ap.	Look, that's how it is also done.

Putting the information on the *ma'm'aga* together with that from the wine feast we see that both rites involve a kind of hunting and a kind of harvesting. The wine feast had a rabbit hunt. So far as we know no ritual precautions were attached to it. The rabbits were simply food. There were precautions with the deer—how it must be killed, who must cook it, and that it must be cooked without salt. It appears that the special treatment of the deer was needed to make farm crops safe to eat, and not vice versa. Deer could be killed and eaten at any time but the crops were something special. Their existence was more closely tied to human society and their fruition depended on the summer rains which mankind obtained through the wine feasts. We recall the lines of wine feast oratory:

On top of that (land) something (crops) came out
It thought it came out by itself
Then got nice and ripe (Running Speech).

Is there a corresponding harvest in the wine feast? Yes, it is the cactus harvest. There are differences between the two harvests. Cactuses are not planted by people and, more importantly, they come into fruit without rain. This, then, is the whole sequence:

June—saguaros ripen almost by magic before the rains while the earth is parched and dry.

July—more or less simultaneously the rains begin, the cactus harvest is held, the wine feasts are held, and the crops are planted.

August—the rains continue, the crops grow.

September—the *ma'a'aga*, the first crops are harvested, and the rains stop.

Is there a concern over sickness at the wine feast comparable to the concern over diarrhoea at the *ma'm'aga*? Yes, the same sickness. The drinking of wine gives people diarrhoea, not by accident but on purpose. After drinking a certain amount (the amounts are large as the wine is served in large baskets) one begins to vomit, that is, one begins to empty himself via the mouth. This result is as certain as night following day. After a longer period of drinking, the purging process moves into the bowels producing diarrhoea.

The diarrhoea and vomiting share this feature, that their "victim" does not keep his nourishment but passes it out in the form of liquid. By drinking cactus wine people put themselves in more or less the same condition as the summer rain clouds, bursting forth with liquids. This connection is explicit, for Underhill was told about the vomitting, "Look, he's throwing up clouds" (1946:67).

The *ma'm'aga* is meant to bring this condition to a close. Of course it is not that mankind has had diarrhoea continually since the wine feast. There may have been other rites in the meantime, especially the salt pilgrimage, and weeks and months of normal toil. But on the symbolic level, the cleaning of the crops closes what the wine feast opened, the "liquid" portion of the year.

Underhill learned that a very similar sickness comes from the ocean. It is called 'yellow vomit' (1946:241-42). This is a sickness, however, not a natural consequence of engaging in the salt pilgrimage. It is said to affect people who were careless during the pilgrimage. It is also said to come from the smell of the ocean itself—the bitter, salty small. (Apaches are said to smell the same way and to produce the same effects—1946:242).

We next take up the *ma'm'aga* as Underhill recorded it from Kaka village, beginning with the speeches. These were used in the first and third phases, the same as at Santa Rosa. The speeches below were recorded from Happy Jim according to Underhill's records, a man whose English name may have been a play on the Papago *ha-bijim*, 'turns them around'.

SPEECH TO INITIATE DEER HUNT

Happy Jim, Kaka

Aheu'u, mant heg ñ-omhaidag cem ñei, t heki hu a i s-e-wia	Yes, I looked upon my buckskin, it was already all worn out
Kunt hegai ñ-giadag am cem ñei, t heki hu a i s-e-wia	I looked upon my bowstring, it was already all worn out
Am cem ñei g ñ-uwiga, t heki hu a i s-e-wia eñiga	I looked upon my women, already worn out were their clothes
Eḍa cegitok am ma:sk o wuak am taccui.	Then it was remembered and it appeared and happened as desired.

Im huḍuñig wui wo:gk na:to kc wua g s-cuk ba'ag, am oidk ke:ṣwa g s-tonlig ñ-we:mgal	Towards the sunset [I] made a road and placed the black eagle, beyond that placed my shining helper [coyote]
Im ka:cim wui wo:gk na:to, ke:ṣwa g s-cuk ba'ag, am oidk ke:ṣwa g s-tonlig ñ-we:mgal	Towards the sea [south] made a road, placed the black eagle, beyond that placed my shining helper
Im si'alig wui wo:gk na:to, ke:ṣwa g s-cuk ba'ag, am oidk ke:ṣwa g s-tonlig ñ-we:mgal	Towards the morning [east] made a road, placed the black eagle, beyond that placed my shining helper
Im wiñim wui wo:gk na:to, ke:ṣwa g s-cuk ba'ag, am oidk ke:ṣwa g s-tonlig ñ-we:mgal.	Towards the north made a road, placed the black eagle, beyond that placed my shining helper.
A'ai wo:pok mia hegai huawi	Back and forth they ran and neared the deer
Am hihink g we:mgal am i ge:ṣk am bañmeḍ	There howled the helper, there he [deer] fell and crawled
T am mel g o'odham, bei, ha'ap o mo'ocudk woi huḍuñig wui	There a man ran up, took it [deer], laid its head to the sunset
Am bei g bahijk me: u:pam	Took its tail and ran homewards
Gḍ hu meli g ma:kai o'odham	Arrived running [with it] at the medicine man
Am daha, am cupulim s-cukca'in, u'apa g bahij, am eḍa ce:	[Medicine man] Sat, marked off a square, took the tail, put it in [the square]
Am ce:mo'o g o'odham, am behi g bahij, we:sko i e-dagyu, hekaj ab e-kulañmad.	Then arrived the people, took the tail, rubbed themselves all over, and that way cured themselves.

SPEECH BEFORE BUTCHERING THE DEER

Happy Jim, Kaka

Aheu'u, t awa p a e-ju: g ñ-taccui	Yes, my wish was done
O wa wuḍ g ṣawad k wa'ukaj hekaj hemajkamcudk na:to	There was the thick straw, with it a person [I] made and finished it
O wa wuḍ g kikihoḍ, nt ab kakiotat	There were the rainbows, I made them be hind legs
Wuḍ g to:mug, kunt ab no:nhotat	There was the milky way, I made it be forelegs
Wuḍ g hewel, kunt a hekaj we:sko i dagyu, amjeḍ i a'akim	There was the wind, I rubbed it all over, then it [the deer that was being made] dripped
Wuḍ g ṣawad wa'ukaj, kunt ag ab i mo:toi	There was the thick straw, I put it on the head [as horns]
S-taḍañ ha:hakaj, kunt ag ab na:nkaj	There were the broad leaves, I put them on it as ears
Kunt g hewel i kapicka, ab u:ṣapkaj	And the wind I folded, put it on it as a snout

K wuḍ g cia, kunt ag ab wu:puic	There was the hail, I made it into eyes
Wuḍ g hewel, nt ag hekaj we:sko i dagyu, amjeḍ i a'akim	There was the wind, I rubbed it all over, then it dripped
K wuḍ g ce:wagi, nt am a:t da:m ce:k dagṣ	And there was the cloud, I put it on it for buttocks and pressed it
Kunt ab wo:potatk dagito.	Then I made hair for it and let it go.
Kut g do'ag, kut g s-cuk hodaidag am da:k heg baṣo ab cu:dowa k g s-komagi do'ag heg we:gaj am ke:k	There was a mountain, over its black rocks it [deer] jumped and in front of it danced, and behind a grey mountain it stood
Am we:gaj ke:k g u'us s-hiosig	Behind that stood a flowering tree
Eḍa g we:gaj has cu'ig g wiapio ke'el, am wuak am si:ckowa	Behind that were my grown boys, they threw it down and wounded it
C am meli g ñ-keli, ñ-wiapo, ñ-aliga, hekaj ab i dagyu, ab ta:ñ g s-keg duakag.	Then ran up my old man, my boy, my child, they rubbed themselves with it [deer tail], they asked for a good life.

The hero of these speeches does not travel. Let us consider what he does instead. In the first speech he puts out animals to assist him in finding the deer: A black coyote and a shining eagle are placed in each of the four directions. We have seen blackness and shininess associated with opposed directions, west and east, in the salt pilgrimage speeches. Here both colors are apportioned to all four directions. It is not said where the deer was found—it is as if the four pairs converged to find him. Once killed, the deer was laid out by humans with the head to the west and tail to the east. The tail was sent home to a medicine man and used by people to cure themselves. The word we translate as 'cure' is *kulañmad*, literally 'to apply medicine'.

We may interpret the color references in this speech as follows: When directions are distinguished as to color, it is because mankind, represented by the hero, wants something from that direction. The variously colored clouds of the mockingbird speeches illustrate this principle. We will see further examples of it in the *a'ada* speech and the *I'itoi* speech, below. In the present speech the hero sends his agents in the four directions. His own color is constant (speeches never say what color a human hero is; presumably he is the color of a normal Papago) and so are the colors of his agents.

We call the hero of this speech human, but he is better endowed than most humans. The speech begins with him in need of leather but well endowed with helpers. Hunting is not difficult for such a hero. He need only set out his coyotes and eagles. It is recalled that Coyote figured into the Anegam "B" salt pilgrimage speech, at the end of a black road, but coyotes play a different role here. There he was a 'made father' host to the hero, here they are extensions of the hero's will. If we envision "man" and "god" on a scale or a continuum of powers, then this hero falls farther along the scale towards godhood than the heroes of the wine feast or salt pilgrimage speeches. Perhaps this is why he does not travel. As a god, he has agents to travel for him.

Turning now to the second speech, we note that it, too, lacks a journey by the hero. Two thirds of the speech is a preface telling what the hero did before anyone started to travel. He did a remarkable thing. He made a deer. Viewing the two speeches as a progression, we may conclude that this hero is even better endowed than the first one. He is more a god than a normal man, for he can produce the animal that men are about to hunt. He seems all the more godlike in the light of the preceding chapters, for he produced the deer from wet weather and green vegetation, two of the most precious things of the Papago universe.

The portion of the speech devoted to the hunt is as brief and effortless as in the first speech. We note that both texts end with people rubbing themselves with parts of the killed deer. This act is similar to the application of "power" in the salt pilgrimage. The first Kaka speech phrases this rubbing as a kind of medication, and the second speech phrases it as a wish for a 'good life'. We will interpret this wish below, after sketching rituals at Kaka and Pisinimo.

At Kaka the deer was used in essentially the same way as at Santa Rosa. Before returning to the village the tail was cut off and passed over each man, just as the first hunting speech describes. Once transported home, the meat was cooked without salt by old women. This was done on the day of the hunt. There was no *a'ada* to remove sickness from the entire village.

As at Santa Rosa, the meat was cleaned with thorny cholla cactus branches, and fresh crops were brought to the ritual ground for cleaning. During the dance in the night, women painted their bodies to represent corn and men carried hunting arrows. Again, the overall explanation is that the deer was killed to make the new farm crops nourishing.

The Pisinimo ceremony as described by Underhill appears similar to those discussed above, only it involves the use of a ceremonial bundle as well as the killing of a deer. This bundle was kept in the mountains at some distance from the village. On the day of the hunt, some men went to fetch the bundle while the others went to hunt the deer. At the nighttime dance, the bundle was placed at the far eastern end of a line of ceremonial objects, the entire line being situated on an east-west axis in front of (that is, east of) the round house. Immediately west of the bundle was a tuft of eagle down feathers that had been stored in the ceremonial bundle. These feathers are associated with clouds and with rain. West of the feathers was a cholla branch which, in Pisinimo as in the other villages, was used to purify the meat. West of the cholla branch was an ironwood stake which would be used at the end of the rite to drive the collected impurities into the ground. We will see an ironwood stake used in the same way in the Santa Rosa *a'ada*. When the rite was finished, after the sickness had been disposed of and the meat had been eaten, the eagle down tuft was returned to the basket. The basket was closed and the deer's tail was passed around it. The basket was then returned to the mountains.

Putting the available information from the three villages together at this point, we see the following elements: A deer is killed. People rub themselves with parts of it immediately. Later they purify the meat with cholla branches. They purify their new crops in the same manner. At least three different things happen to parts of the deer. Its flesh is eaten—it enters into people. Its "impurities" are removed and driven into the ground. Finally, its tail (and probably its bones as well) are sent back to the mountains. Only the first two things happen to the crops.

The second speech provides our best clue into the logic of those happenings. The god who is the hero of that speech produced meat from moisture and green plants. Mankind would like to duplicate this feat within their own stomachs, that is, to transform their farm crops into flesh. This is to suggest that the deer is viewed as a strict vegetarian and the animal kingdom's counterpart to a farmer, a specialist in (wild) plants.

On this interpretation, the rubbing at the end of the hunt is a rubbing with a "transformed" deer, one whose flesh has been formed from moisture and greens. The wish for a good life is for a life made fleshy from the vegetal matter of crops. Let us interpret one more detail. The rule against shedding the deer's blood may be seen on one level as a rule against spilling its fluids, but it also harks back to the saguaro harvest. The pulp of the fresh cactus fruits is red and the fruits themselves are called 'hearts'. The spilling of this blood and its wholesale drinking as wine is what makes it rain. The sparing of the deer's blood and the eating of its "magic" flesh is meant to stop that process. For the rest of the year, if the work was done well, mankind will be able to live off its crops.

The last recorded variation on the *ma'm'aga* is from Quitovac, Sonora. Here the watery qualities of the deer apparently are used in making it rain, not in ushering in the dry season. At Quitovac the deer hunt is held earlier than at the other villages, in August, within the rainy season. The hunt is combined with a large and impressive rite called *wi:gita* which is held at only one other place, on a ritual ground shared by Santa Rosa, Ak Chin, Anegam, and Sil Nagia (Ge Aji). The latter "northern" *wi:gita* is held in November, normally after the *ma'm'aga*; the "southern" version is held twelve days after the *ma'm'aga*. The Quitovac *wi:gita* includes the making of wine. Thus within the space of about a month (counting preparations, etc.), this southern Papago tradition combines elements of what in the north are three rituals which spread over a five month period (July to November).

It is apparent that the *wi:gita*, *ma'm'aga*, and wine feast are pieces of farming ritual which have crystalized differently in different villages. The *wi:gita* is a harvest ceremony just as the *ma'm'aga* is. We do not discuss either version of it in this book because we have no speeches from them. The use of wine to make rain at the Quitovac ceremony seems to collapse the distinction in the north between celebrating the onset and the close of the rainy season. A close examination of the setting of this ceremony might yield the reasons why: that Pithaya rather than saguaro cactus fruits are harvested for the wine and the pithaya season is later, that the farming at this location is on a different schedule from the farming of the northern villages, etc. We must leave these issues, having only touched the tips of them, because the information on the Quitovac rite is quite sketchy and, as was stated above, we lack speeches from it.

A'ADA

We come to the final of the three rites involving hunting, the *a'ada*. The information is from Santa Rosa, and we have a speech. The word *a'ada* means 'the sending'. The idea is that sickness is sent away. *A'ada*s can be performed either as part of a *ma'm'aga* rite, analogous to the inclusion of a rabbit hunt within the time span of a wine feast, or they can be performed on their own. We will discuss the combined form first. In this case, on the day after the hunters' return, and prior to the night of dancing, the men of the village visit every house to dislodge and collect sickness. The sickness is dislodged by beating on the outside of the houses with long thorny sticks of ocotillo, rather like beating on a rug. Once knocked loose, the sickness is collected with "jumping cholla" branches, surely one of the stickiest plants known to man. The cleansing takes all day. The sickness collected from the houses is disposed of in the same manner and perhaps at the same time as the sickness collected from the food. It is buried or driven into the ground. The cholla branches are burned. The speech written below is given after the sickness has been collected but before it is disposed of. The version of the speech that we give is from Jose Pancho. It is essentially the same speech as Underhill recorded from Jose Moreno in the 1930s.

Ocotillo. Photo by Karl W. Luckert.

A'ADA SPEECH

Jose Pancho, Santa Rosa

Do: wa'i, ant a hebai ab si ha-i: m g ñ-wiapo'oke'el.	Ready, I have someplace called kinship to my young men.
Ant a am ceṣajig wui g s-toha wo: gidk na: to	Towards the sunrise I made the white road and finished
Tag oidk gi'ik ab ṣoṣ g ñ-wiapo'oke'el	Along it my grown boys make four stops
Ta ab si ce: mo'o g s-toha melhog.	Reach the white ocotillo.
Ba cem pi ba: bagi ta-ji: wim kaij	It is not to be approached slowly [according to how] it sounds
Am eḍa ab si kuhuk am eḍa ab si bebedk am eḍa ab si duahi, am eḍa ab si si: s	Inside it really hoots, inside it really rumbles, inside it really thunders, inside it really sizzles
Tag we: gaj gi'iko on i bij	There around it four times they circle
Ceṣajig ta: gio ma: hakaj tab muliñk im u'apa	The sunrise direction branch they break and carry off
T hekaj g ha'icu has ta: hadkam si kuawid si: ṣk na: to	With it the bad feelings they nail down flat and finish.
Ant a im t-na: nki ta: gio ge s-wegi wo: gidk na: to	In the north direction I made the red road and finished
Kut ag oid gi'ik ab ṣoṣ g ñ-wiapo'oke'el	Along it my grown boys make four stops
Ab si ce: mo'o g s-wegiom melhog.	Reach the red ocotillo.
Tag eḍa cem pi ba: bagi ta-ji: wim kaij	It is not to be approached slowly it sounds
Am eḍa ab si bebedk am eḍa ab si kuhuk am eḍa ab si duwahi, am eḍa ab si si: s	Inside it really rumbles, inside it really hoots, inside it really thunders, inside it really sizzles
Kut ag we: gaj gi'iko on i bijimk	There around it four times they circle
Ka wa t-na: nki ta: gio ma: hakaj tab muliñk im u'apa	The north direction branch they break and carry off
K hekaj g ha'icu has ta: hadkam si kuawid si: ṣk na: to.	With it the bad feelings they nail down flat and finish.
Do: wa'i, ant a am ka: cim wui ge s-ta: tki wo: git	Ready, in the south direction I made the glossy road and finished
Tag oid gi'ik ab ṣoṣ g ñ-wiapo'oke'el	Along it my grown boys make four stops
K ab si ce: mo'o g s-ta: tki melhog.	Reach the glossy ocotillo.
K eḍa cem pi ba: bagi ta-ji: wim kaij	It is not to be approached slowly it sounds
Am eḍa ab si bebedk am eḍa ab si kuhuk am eḍa ab si duwahi, am eḍa ab si si: s	Inside it really rumbles, inside it really hoots, inside it really thunders, inside it really sizzles
Kut ag we: gaj gi'ikho on i bij	There around it four times they circle
Ka ag ka: cim ta: gio ma: hakaj kut ag muliñk im u'apa	The south direction branch they break and carry off

Jumping cholla cactus. Photo by Karl W. Luckert.

T hekaj g ha'icu has ta:hadkam si
kuawid si:ṣk na:to.

Ant a im huḍuñig wui g s-cuk wo:gidk
na:to
Kut ag oid gi'ik ab ṣoṣ g ñ-wiapo'oke'el
Ab si ce:mo'o g s-cuk melhog.
Eḍa cem pi ba:bagi ta-ji:wim kaij
K am eḍa ab si bebedk am eḍa ab si
kuhuk am eḍa ab si duwahi, am eḍa
ab si si:s
Kut ag we:gaj gi'ikho on i bij
K ag huḍuñig ta:gio ma:hakaj kut ag
muliñk im u'apa
Hekaj g ha'icu has ta:hadkam si kuawid
si:ṣk na:to

Do:wa'i, t haha i wu:ṣ g s-cuk hiañ
ma:kai
At ag jeweḍ gi'ikpa am si ki'iwink ha'icu
has ta:hadkam i na:si
K g eḍa am si ba:bagi ṣo cem si hugiok
e-a:.

With it the bad feelings they nail down
flat and finish.

In the west direction I made the black
road and finished
Along it my grown boys make four stops
Reach the black ocotillo.
It is not to be approached slowly it sounds
Inside it really rumbles, inside it really
hoots, inside it really thunders, inside
it really sizzles
There around it four times they circle
The west direction branch they break
and carry off
With it the bad feelings they nail down
flat and finish.

Ready, then emerged the black tarantula
medicine man
The earth he four times chewed and the
bad feelings he folded up
They slowed and seemed almost to finish.

Do:wa'i, t haha i wu:ṣ ge s-wepeg ku:g bibiakam ma:kai	Ready, then emerged the red end circling medicine man [an insect]
At ag jeweḍ gi'ik am si haha'atk na:tok ha'icu has ta:hadkam i na:si	Dirt he four times made into a jar and finished and the bad feelings he folded up
K g eḍa am ba:bagi k am cem si hugiok e-a:.	Inside it they slowed and seemed almost to finish.
Ta i hu t-da:mjeḍ i huḍ ge s-gewk a'anam u'uhig	Then from above descended the strong winged bird
At ag hejel e-macwuidag hupañk am a'ai si gewkamiok am cem si hugiok e-a:.	His own wing feather he plucked and back and forth beat with it and seemed almost to finish.
Do:wa'i, at haha i wu:ṣ g has ali koṣkam hemajkam	Ready, and then emerged the little sleeping people [ants]
To ha ñ-ki: eḍ i wa:pk ha'icu ñ-hugi ab i bebbehi, ñ-ceṣandag ab i bebbehi, ñ-wawandag ab i bebbehi, ñ-ki:kio ab i bebbehim	They entered my house and took from my food, took from my house posts, took from my rafters, took from my wall straighteners
K at ju:piñ hewel wui si a'ad.	To the north wind they really sent it [sickness].
Do:wa'i, t a in hu cem al wi'i	Ready, now a little still remains
At haha i huḍ g s-wa: ka:cim	Then the moisture from above starts to fall
K eḍa am si wi'umk na:to.	It will ruin it and finish.
Ñe: ha'ap ampt hems i elidk o taccu, nanko ñ-i:m.	Look, thus you may wish and plan, my various relatives.

The speech has a stationary hero like the previous two *ma'm'aga* speeches. It mentions ocotillo as a means for disposing of the sickness ('bad feelings'), but mentions a number of other means as well: tarantula medicine man, 'end circling medicine man' (flying insect which is so named because it is often seen circling around the ends of tree branches), a bird, ants, and a mysterious moisture from the sky. While the means are mysterious, the effects are not. Little by little the sickness is obliterated.

It is noted that the ocotillo is described as an object alive with moisture. It rumbles and thunders inside. The words used to describe this plant are equally descriptive of thunderclouds (mockingbird speeches), the ocean (Anegam "B" speech), and an upset stomach. Here a plant with those qualities is used to combat a sickness with the same qualities.

We turn now to the other context of the *a'ada* which is to cleanse a village outside the harvest season. In this case there is no *ma'm'aga*. The most commonly stated cause for sickness in this case is evil medicine men from other villages. They send 'poison' *(hiwhoina)* enclosed in a small tube (Underhill, 1946:281). The tube lodges itself somewhere within the ground of the victim village. People begin to feel the effects of the poison. These may include a host of problems besides diarrhoea. A medicine man from the home village is called to locate the poison and extract it.

The medicine man's work for this *a'ada* is strictly parallel to his work for a deer hunt. He works through the night to the accompaniment of other people's singing. As was remarked earlier, this is nearly a constant feature in Papago rituals. We saw it in the wine feast and the salt pilgrimage and we will see it again in the war campaign. Only the object of his search changes, and the placement of this event within the entire ritual sequence. May we then add poison tubes to the list of objects sought in ceremonial journeys? We may, with the realization that

Sending sickness away during an *a'ada* rite. Drawing by Mike Chiago

the journey aspect is here reduced to nothing as the participants do not leave the village. Their purpose is not to get something from nature to bring into human society, but to remove an unwanted thing from human society (sickness) and send it back to nature—at least to get rid of it.

Once the sickness is located, usually near dawn, the medicine man goes to extract and destroy it. Then the rest of the *a'ada* proceeds as usual. Ocotillo sticks and cholla branches are used to extract sickness from every house, the idea being that a good deal of poison has escaped from the hidden tube. At the end of the day, this collected sickness is disposed of with the *a'ada* speech.

War

With the war campaign, called *gidahim*, we reenter the realm of 'made fathers' and power. The time is early winter, after the crops are in. Before we discuss the rite we must note that it is the one winter ritual treated in this book. It stands alone in the approximately seven month period between 'Dry grass moon' (the *ma'm'aga*) and the spring rites of our final chapter which fall around May. The year's ceremonialism seems concentrated around the summer rains.

Were the seven "dry" months really empty? On the Native side there was the northern *wi:gita* mentioned in the last chapter. These were also many "social dances" and foot races at this time—winter was a time of social pleasures. Finally there was the telling of the creation story around the winter solstice. There are also numerous Christian rituals between October and May: a major pilgrimage to Magdalena, Sonora, Mexico, All Souls' Day, Christmas, Lent, and Easter. By the late nineteenth century these Christian rites were firmly a part of Papago life.

The notion of an "empty" seven month dry season is therefore an artifact of this book. One may add the further corrections that the period from October to May was not necessarily dry as there are the winter rains discussed in the Ocean chapter; that *ma'm'agas* might be held in November; or there might be winter salt pilgrimages. All that having been said, there remains a fundamental fact that the "dry season" rites, Native and Christian, were dependent on the summer rains and planting season. If the work of that season went well, there would be food to sustain concentrations of people for social dances, to support a pilgrimage to Magdalena, or to gamble on footraces. If the wet season work did not go well, people would disperse and live on short rations. To sum up, the "wet season" rituals laid the foundation for all that would follow.

What we know of war fits with the above characterization. Papago wars were planned in advance and involved large concentrations of people, especially for the celebrations of the final phase. A full fledged war campaign is the longest and most complex ritual described in this book. From beginning to end it could take a month and involve hundreds of people from several villages. This would be a war in a rich year.

As with the salt pilgrimage, we are fortunate to have an account of the war campaign by a participant. He is Baptisto Lopez of Santa Rosa. Mr. Lopez is a *siakam*, a word we translate as '(war) hero'. He became one in the 1950s when Santa Rosa, Ak Chin, Anegam, and Sil Nagia (Ge Aji) last put on a war campaign against 'straw' enemies, that is, enemies made of straw by the old men for the purpose of initiating young men into the status of *siakam*. The last "real" raids were in the late 1800s against the Apaches.

We will begin with this first hand account of the *gidahim* and follow with a general discussion of the rite and its speeches. Mr. Lopez's account was taped in Papago for this book in the spring of 1978. It was not rehearsed and like all personal narratives, it could have been expanded in some places and diminished in others. We give it in Papago and in English. The reader will see a strong similarity between it and Brennan's written narrative on the salt pilgrimage.

WAR CAMPAIGN

Baptisto Lopez, Santa Rosa

I:da	This
Keli o'odham	Old people
Mat hab masma am b o i elidad	When they will be thinking
Mat hab o o ju:	That they will do
Gidahim	The war campaign
Am hemajkam ha-we:hejeḍ	For the people
Am e-jeweḍga we:hejeḍ	For their land
No pi wuḍ si ha'icu	Because it is important
Mat o hekajkad hegai	For them to use that
Mat hab masma o melc g s-ta:hadkam	So they can bring pleasure
Am e-hejel e-we:hejeḍ	To themselves
E-ki:dag we:hejeḍ	To their society
We:s hemajkam ha-ki:dag we:hejeḍ.	To everyone's society.
Hab masma mo in i ha'icug	That's how it is around here
Gogo'olkol ki:dag hab masma, ñe:	There are separate towns, look
Mo iya ha'icug kaij me:k am o'odham	Here are the Santa Rosa people
C ab ha'icug aki ciñ ab o'odham	And there are the Ak Chin people
C ab ha'icug sil nagiak ab o'odham	And there are the Sil Nagia people
C in ha'icug a:ngam an o'odham.	And there are the Anegam people.
Pegi, t g hemajkam o taccuk	Well, and the people want it
Am ha-wui gei	It falls to them
Am ha-wui hegam	To those
Man i ka'akwuḍko ki:dag	Of the several towns
K am g ha-ba'ic i hihimdam i hemajkam	And their later generations.
Ab o ha-waidk	They will call them
Am o daḍiya am e-wui	They will sit facing them
K am o a'aga i:da	And will tell them this
Mat hascu ḍ o i hegaik	That something will take place
Mat g hekaj am o i ha-wai.	And that is why they called them.

Am o e-we:m ñenokk
Am o je:ñig
To o-na:to hegai.

They will talk to each other
They will hold a meeting
That's what they will do.

Pegi, k ab aha wo ha i ha-ma: hegam,

Well, and then they will give it [news] to them,

Kutp a'i o bekk hi: g ha'icu a:ga

The announcement will be carried this way and that

K an o wa a:gi g e-hemajkam
Mat hascu am i na.to
Am we:hejeḍ g e-ki:dag, e-jeweḍga
Mat g hekaj o he:kigculid g e-jeweḍga
Heg hekaj ab ab o i cem bei g e-we:mtadag.

Thus they will tell their own people
That something was done
Concerning their social life, their land
Through which their land will be happy
Through which they will get their help.

Pegi, k hab masma hab cu'ig
Mat an haha wo e-hemapa g e-ki:dagk e-hemajkamga
K am o ke:k g ki:
Mat g eḍa am o e-hemapadk
Am o s-mai
Matp hascu am wuḍ a'i hegaikad.

Well, and that's how it is
Then they will gather their town and their people
A house stands there [round house]
In which they will gather
To find out
What it is that will take place.

Pegi, k am o e-hemapadk
Am s-mai
Mo ki hascu hab elidag g t-wañmeḍdam

Well, and they will gather
And will find out,
"There must be something our leader wants

Mat ki hascu ab o t-a:gid
K hascu ab o t-kakke ab ab hegai
Mat o s-ap'ekad hegai.

Something he will tell us
Something he will ask us about
If it will be all right."

Pegi, k ab o wa ha-ab
Matp he'ekiac am o ha'icug
Matp hab o cei
"A:ñi ant am o him"
K hema e:p, hema e:p.

Well, and it will be up to them
As many as will be present
That they will say,
"I, I'll go there [to war]"
And somebody else, and somebody else.

Pegi, no pi am a s-ap'e
Mo om b e-elid hegai
K ab o i e-nako ab e-ṣoiga aba'i
Ha'icu e-eñiga abai
Matp he'es i an hab o i ju:.
A'an matp o eḍagidc
He'es am hab o i ju:
Am i wonami abai hegai
O eḍagid g e-ga:t
Ho u'ad hegai
Matp has i ma:s wuḍ o ga:t

Well, because it is proper
For someone to think on it
To get his horse ready for it
Or something else that he owns
As much as he has to do.
Feathers if he has them
As much as he has to do
Or make a hat
Or if he has a gun
He will bring it
Whatever kind of gun it is

O eḍagid g e-la : ns	Or he may have a lance
Mat g o hekaj	If that is what he uses
O eḍagid g e-pistol	Or he may have a pistol
Mat g o hekaj	If that is what he uses
O eḍagid g e-u : s ga:t	Or he may have a bow
Matp o hekaj.	If he uses that.
Pegi, k am o ḍ a'i hegai	Well, so it must be
Mat am b o cei	When they will say
Mo om a s-ap'e	That it is all right
Mat am o a : g taṣ	They will announce the day
Mat he'ekia wuḍ	As many as it will be
Gi'ik tas.	Four days.
Pegi k heki hu u-na : to	Well, and it is ready
We : s ha'icu ab e-na : toc	Everything is ready
Mat hascu e-wa'igi	Whatever will be brought as liquid
Mat g o i : 'et	So one can drink it
Man o hasko nagiacugad	So he will have it hanging there [on his horse]
Ha'icu e-cu'iṣpa a hebai an ep nagiacugad	Something for lunch will also be hanging there
Mat g hekaj o hi : amai.	So he can use it in going there.
Pegi k g we : s am e-na : tokc heki hu	Well, and everything is ready
C hab masma hab cu'ig hegai	That's how it is
Mat hekid o i e-ai g taṣ	That the day will come
Kut am o i e-hemapa amai	They will gather there
Mo hebai ha'icug g ha-u : gcu'u	Where their leader is
Pegi, k t hekid o i e-na : tok o hi : .	Well, and when they are ready they go.
We : sko a'ai da : kam hemajkam	All the different village people
A : ngam anai kut ab o i hihim	At Anegam they will start out
K g sil nagiak amjeḍ	And from Sil Nagia
Aki ciñ amjeḍ	From Ak Chin
C i amjeḍ	And from here
Pegi t am o hihimk o e-nam amai	Well, they will go and will meet there
Mat hebai o ap'ecudask g jeweḍ.	Where the place has been prepared.
We : sij s-ma : c	Everybody knows
Mat hebai o e-ṇam	Where they will meet
Pegi t am o dada amai	Well, they will meet there
Am o dadak o ho wupuls g e-ṣoṣoiga.	They will arrive and tie up their horses.
Kut am hekihu ji : wia g s-u : gcu'u	The leader will have already arrived
K am haha has o i cei	Soon he will say something
O u'ugcid g e-la : ns k o moihu	[First] He will take his lance and soften
Ha'as e sikolt am o moihu g jeweḍ	For so far around he will soften the earth

He'ekia o i ha-a:g
E-we:m o gegokiak e-we:m o cu'amo
O moihu hegai jeweḍ hegai.

Hekid hema wo jijiwapat
Am o kei g e-la:ns hegai.

Hema g ga.t o u'ad
Ep o kei hegai ga:t
Hema e:p, hema e:p
Hema g pistol o eḍagidc
Ab o nagia
Ga:t ku:g ab o nagia hegai.

Pegi k t hekid o i ji:wia
K am o himk
Gḍ hu o nagia amai
Matp hebai oi i ha'icukad
Am o himk
Ab o dahiya hugid ab hegam
Mat am o daḍaikad hegai.

B masma hab o o-ju:
Im hu wo je:ñgidad hegai
Mo g ha u:gcu'u ha'icukaj o
    ho-je:ñgidad hegai hegam
Mat he'ekiac am o i dada.

Hekid am o i we:s
Hebai o ṣu:d hegai
Mat ab a cu:cia g e-ga:gt
Pegi k t am o i amic
Mat am a we:sij dadahim
Am hab o cei
"Mo om a s-ap'e,
Na as am a we:sij dadahim"
Pegi k t am aha wa ṣonc hegai
    ha-u:gcu'u.

Am hab o cei
"Mapt s-ma:c
Mas has hascukaj i i hihim
Hemu wuḍ hegai
Mac idañ g hekaj hihim
Idañ i i t-hemapad
Ia t-na:to hegai."

He will tell several of them
Will stand together and poke [the earth]
To soften the earth in that way.

Whenever someone arrives
He will stand his lance there.

Someone will bring a gun
He'll also stand the gun
Someone else, someone else
Someone will have a pistol
He will hang it
On the end of the [rifle] gun he will
    hang it.

Well, and when they arrive
There they go
And hang it over there
Wherever it will be
They go there then
And sit beside them
Who are already sitting there.

Then it will happen
That they will hold a meeting
Their leader will have a meeting about
    something
With as many as will have arrived there.

When they are all there
When the place is full
When they have stood up their guns
Well, then he will understand
That they have all arrived
He will say
"Good,
Apparently everybody has been arriving"
Well, then he will start off.

He will say
"You knew
You started on something
Now this is it
We are going on with it
Now we have gathered
Here we have done it."

Gamai hu wo ñio	On he will talk
Matp has i masma s-e-amicudk o ñio hegai	However he knows how to talk
Pi has o ṣai e-elidad	That they shouldn't worry
Gamai hu wo ho-gewkamhogi hegai.	That this will give them strength.
"Pi has o ṣai elidad	"There's nothing to worry about
Am o ḍ hegai	Only this
Mampt am hugkam o e-gewkamho amai	That you will be strong for one purpose
Matt hebai o i ha-a'ahe hegam t-o:bga	That we will meet enemies someplace
Pi heḍai hab o ṣa'i el	Nobody should think
'Mant u:pam o ha'icu o cikp'	'I have something to do at home'
Im apt o ha'ap o himc g e-gewkdagc ha'icu cegito'idag hegai	You should direct your strength and thought on this side
Wui o hi:	They should go this way
Mat heḍai wuḍ o i hegaikad	Whoever it will be
Mat g wui o hi:"	Who will go this way"
Am o ñiokk o ñio	He'll talk and talk
Am he'ekia s-amicud	As much as he knows
C niokk am o i ku:g hegai.	He'll talk to the end.
T ga hu hasko ki:dagkam g ha-u:gcu'u hegai	Then some other peoples' leader
Aki ciñ, a:ngam, sil nagia	Ak Chin, Anegam, Sil Nagia [villages]
Ep wo ñiok ha-u:gcu'u	Will also talk
"Mọ om a woho hegai	"That's the truth
Kupt am a wui am o himc g ha'icu e-cegito'idag hegai	And you will make your thoughts go in that direction
Pegi t hemhu am b i:ya s-iham o ju:	Of course the arrangements will be made right here
Pt o u:hum o dada hemhua am u:pam"	You'll get home again of course"
B o wa i masma o hihim hegai.	Thus it goes.
Hema ep wo ñiok ga hu ha'ap	Another one will talk after that
Am o i ku:gi	And he will end
T hema ep wo ñio e:p	Someone else will also talk
Ñe: k hab masma o hihi hegai.	Look, and thus it goes.
K hekid am o i ku:gi	And when it is ended
Mat we:sij am o ñeño	When they have all talked
T b aha wo ñiok g t-wanmeḍdam, t-u:gcu'u	Then our leader will talk, our chief
S-hasigkam ñioki hegai	It's a difficult talk, that one
Wui wuḍ o ñiokad hegai	It's for him to talk
C am o ñiok ñio	And he talks and talks
Cew wuḍ o ñioki hegai.	It's a long talk, that one.

K hekid am o i ku:g hegai	When it has ended
T in hugid an da:k	He sits beside them
Ab o i:m	They state their kinship to him
Matp has wuḍ o i juñhidkad	Whatever the relationship is
Pegi k amjeḍ o hi: g i:mig.	Well, and from there starts the kinship telling.
K o him k o him k o him k o him k o him	And it goes and goes and goes and goes and goes
T o i bijim k o him k o him	And it turns and goes and goes
Pegi t o i ji:wia hegai i:mig.	Well, and it will arrive back again, the kinship telling.
Pegi, k pi has cu'igk am o nagia g kawaḍ	Well, and there's nothing wrong with a shield hanging there
Heg at am ep o e-nagia g kawaḍ g ṣoñcki we:nad	With the shield hangs a club
T hema am o ho-ñei	Somebody will sing
Matp am ha'i o ñei.	He will sing a few.
Pi has cu'ig	There's nothing wrong.
Mo heg o hema hab i i-elidad	With somebody wishing
Mo bei g kawaḍk o keihinacud g kawaḍ hegai.	To take the shield and make it dance.
Ñe:, k am aha wa hab o cei "s-ap'e"	Look, they will say "good"
T am o ho-ui hegai e-ga:gt	They will take their guns
Am s-ba:bagi am o ho-ui g ha'icu e-eñiga hegai	Slowly they will take a piece of property
Pi amp ṣ o si i ku:ḍwua wampt o ha'icu i ṣulig hegai	You won't bother it or make something fall
Ba:bagi am o ha-ui	Slowly they will take them
Ga hu u:hum am o i daḍaiya	Later they will set them back again
Mo om heba'i daḍaiya.	Wherever they should be set.
Ñe:, b o wa ju:k ab o i wuwha hegam	Look, they will do and take them out
Mo o-ñiahi	Those [men] who are waiting
Hema am o bebbed id e:p	Somebody will take another one
An ho i dahiya, hema e:p	Then set it back again, and somebody else
S e-juñhimk e-juñhim	They will be doing and doing
To huhugi hi hegai.	It will end of course.
Ha'i g e-lalans am o ho-ui	Some will take their lances
Mat pi o ho-ga:gt	If they don't have guns
C g a'i hekaj hegai e-lalans	And only use their lances
P hascu i u'ad	Whatever they brought
Hehemako ha'icu o u'ad	The separate things they brought
Ne: k am o ui hegai	Look, they will take them
Ga hu wo i daḍaiya.	And later set them back again.

T o huhug amai
T g am o a'i wi: hegai kawaḍc hegai ṣoñci

They will finish there
The shield and the club will remain of course

Im hu wa'i wi'is hegai
Am aha wo ho-a:g
Mat am o ñe'icul hegai
O ñe'iculid g e-kawaḍc e-la:ns
E-ga:gt at o ho-ñe'icul
Ñe:, k am aha wo a:g g ñe'i
Ab o ke:kiwa hegam amai gḍ hu
Ñe:, t am o ho-a:
T o ho-kekaicuna hegam e-ga:gt, e-la:ns.

They will remain there
Then they will tell them
To sing to them
To sing to the shield and lance
To their guns they will sing
Look, and they will sing songs
They will stand over there
Look, they will sing
They will dance their guns and lance.

B o ai matp hema hab o e-elidc
Am o bei hegai kawaḍc hegai ṣoñc
O keihinac hegai ha-we:nadk hegam
Ñe: t hema hab o i e-elid
C hasko ab hema wu:ṣañ
Mo pi ha'icu, al s-we:c ha'icu

Soon someone may wish
To take the shield and club
He will dance with them
Look, and someone may wish
To take it out
If he has nothing very heavy [to dance with]

Mo wu:ṣañk am o bei hegai kawaḍ
Ṣoñcki ep wo bekk wo keihi
Keihiamc hegai.

He will come and take the shield
The club he will also take to dance with
He will pound with it.

Ñe:, k hekid am o i ku:gi hegai
Pegi k t ab aha wa ab o i dagito
Oi an a ha'ap o ho-ui g e-ṣoṣoiga
T o hihim.

Look, and when it ends
Well, they will leave off
Then they will get their horses
And go.

T o i wuwhak im a'ai o hihi
Gḍ hu o ho-ui g e-ṣoṣoiga
K ab o cecedk ab o i e-hemapa
Ha'as i ṣikodim o ke:kiwa
T o hi: hegai ha-ba'ickam
O hi: matp hegai o i s-hi:mim
Matt am o i oi hegam.

They will spring out and scatter
They will get their horses
They will mount them and gather
In a circle they will stand
Their leader will go
He'll go wherever he wants to
And we will follow them.

C amjeḍ hab abṣ o i cu'ig
C abṣ o ho-we:majkad
S o komaḍ hi:
Ha'i kakampañ an o ho-wudacudkad e-ṣoṣoiga ab
Mo kolaikid hegai
Na:nanko masma o e'eniga
K o hihi k o hi:.

Then it will be like this
They will be with him [leader]
They will go in a bunch
Some will have bells on their horses
They will be tinkling
Such are their various properties
And they will go and go.

Hab hu i e-ju: g taṣ	The sun sets
K amjeḍ o hihimk am o hihi	And still they will go and go
Ganai hu wo ai	Finally they'll reach
Mo on wo'oṣañ	Where there are washes
Gn hu hebai ge s-u:gkodag cuwidk	Where there is a high place
Am ep o wu:lṣ g e-ṣoiga g ha-wañmeḍdam	Again their leader will tie his horse
Am o ho-a:g	He will tell them
"Oig o on i ha-wu:lṣpahim g e-ṣoṣoiga	"Go and tie up your horses
Ab ep wo i e-hemapa	Gather up again here
T am ep o i ha-wu:lṣpahi gn hu abṣ me:k g e-ṣoṣoiga."	But tie up your horses again far away."
T am o kegc amai e:p	Then he will clean it [ground] again
Am o ho-a: hegam e-we:mkam	He will tell those who are with him
K o na:to t eḍa im o hihim	Who have finished [tying their horses] and come
Gn hu o i ha-wupulṣpahi	They have tied them off someplace
T eḍa o na:to hegai im hu.	And so they have finished with that.
T am aha ep o kei g e-kawaḍ e:p	Then he will stand up his shield again
Ab ep o nagia g ṣoñci	Again he will hang up his club
Ne: t ab amjeḍ hab ep o ha-cu:cia hegai	Look, and again they will stand up their weapons
B a masma hab ep o ju:.	That's what they will do again.
Am ep o ho-je:ñgi e:p	He will have a meeting with them again
B a masma am ep wo hi: g je:ñgid	This is how the meeting will go
"Idañ hemu i him	"Now we have arrived here
Pi has o ṣa'i elid	There is nothing to worry about
T o a'ahe hegam."	We will reach them [enemies]."
Hab a cu'ig	It is like that
Mat g oidkam we:sij hab o cei ab amjeḍ	That everything will be said about it [by a medicine man]
Matp hema he'es i cew o s-amicuda	If there is someone whose understanding can go that far
An hab o cei hegai.	And he will speak.
Hascu am o i bei am oidahim	He [medicine man] will have gotten something along the way
Heg we:s o o-a:g	And he will tell it all
Ha'ap masma hab cu'igk	How it is
Wuḍ si ha'icu.	And it is really something.
"Kumpt o o-na:ko	"You can make it
Ha'icu gḍ hu wo bei gḍ hu"	You will get something over there."
He'es ha'icu am b o cei	Everything like that he will say
Ñe:, t am o ka:.	Look, and they will listen.

Hab o cei
"Pegi k oi am has ep o i e-ju:"
Ep o ho-ñe'icul e:p hegai
Ha-cucki g ha-i:bdag hegam o:bta
Pi am hu wo ul g ha'icu ha-cegitoidag

He will say
"Well, there is something else to do"
Again they will sing for them
To darken the hearts of their enemies
So they won't keep anything in their minds

Pi ab o ṣa'i kaijid
"B o ha'i hihimc wuḍ t-cegiakam."

So they won't be able to say
"Somebody is coming and it is our enemy."

Pi ab o ṣa'i kaijid
S am o daḍakadc pi ha'icu o ṣa'i ma:c
Eḍa im o hịmad g ha-cegiakam.

They won't be able to say it
They will just sit and not know anything
Yet their enemies will be coming.

Bo ho kaij hegai
O ho-wopojida hegai
Mat o hep hu wua g ha-cegitoidag hegam
Pi ha'icu o ṣa'i ma:c.

He [medicine man] will say that
He will bewitch them
So they will lose their minds
And not know anything.

B o elidadad mo abs am b a'i cu'ig
Pi ha'icu am wuḍ o hegai
Eḍa ab o hihimad hegam
Am b e-ñe'iculid hegai
Ha-kekaicunad g e-ga:gt
Ha-cuckagid hegai.

They [enemies] will think it is like that
That there isn't anything [dangerous]
Yet they [war party] will be coming
As they sing for them
As they pound with their guns
To make them go dark.

Pegi, heg am b a'aga hegai
T eḍa o huḍ g taṣ
B o cei mat am ep o ho-ui hegai

Well, they will sing that [songs]
Yet the sun is setting
So he will say for them to get them [guns and horses] again

T am hik ep o ṣa'i hihimhi
K am hebai ab o i dada.

Once again they will be traveling along
Until they arrive someplace.

Pegi, k am ep hihim
T gm hu ep o ap'ec e:p hegai

T am ep wo dada e:p we:s.

Well, and they will go again
And again they will fix it [the place where they arrive]
Again they will all arrive there.

B o masma hab ep o o-ju:
Mat am ep wo ñio
T a hekaj wuḍ o waikk

Thus they will do it again
Again there will be speeches
Because there are three [stops on the way to the enemy]

Matp am e-na.to
Amjed ab hihim
Kia ep e-na:to
Wuḍ a waikk.

For them to finish
After that they go
And do it again
It is the third.

T hab a masma am ep e-je:ñig e:p hegai	Thus they have another meeting
Ñe:, k b a masma am ep o ju: e:p	Look, because it must be done still another time
Ñe:, k amjeḍ am ep o hi:	Look, and so they go again
T wuḍ o i ha-oidckam hegai.	But that is the last one.
Ga hu hebai atp o o-na:to hegam	Far off someplace they will do it [again]
Ñe:, t am o hihim	Look, and they go
T ab heki hu hema wo i me: hegai	But already one of them has run there
Matp hebai ap'ec g jeweḍ hegai	Wherever the [next] place will be
Meḍk i hu wo ai	He will run and will reach it
Wo nam hegai mo d wañmeḍdam	He will meet with the leader
Ho namk ab we:maj o hi:.	He will meet him and travel with him.
Am ha'ap wo i bei amai	Thus he will take him there
Mat wuḍ a'i gi'ik	Because there must be four [stops]
Ñe:, t am o dada	Look, and they will arrive
T eḍa o s-cuk	But by then it is dark
T am ep o dada.	When they arrive again.
T am heki hu o ol e-na:to	It [the place] will be ready
Heki hu o ui g ku'agi	Already wood will be brought there
No pi abṣ am ge s-ku'agig	Because there is a lot of wood around there
Mo nai.	For them to make a fire.
Pegi, k am o ho-u'apa amai	Well, they will take them [rest of the war party]
T hab o wa ep ha-a:g	They will tell them again
Mo om a heki hu ha-a:g i hu	As they already have told them before
Pegi, t am aha wo ha-wu:pulṣ g e-ṣoṣoiga	Well, and then they tie up their horses
S-winam o ho-wu:pulṣ	Tie them tightly
K am o s-ap i tua hegai.	And then put it [what they have brought] down.
Pegi, k am haha wo ho-a:gi g ha-u:gcu'u	Then their leader will tell them
"I:ya ha wa i s-ap'e	"Here it is proper
I wuḍ a'i i:da	It has to be here
Matt i o wua g t-huḍuñig.	That we will spend our evening.
O ma:sid t ab o ṣul	It will dawn and you will fall
Ma:sid t o wa cegia	It will dawn and you will fight
Kut hekaj hab o o-ju:	Since that is the reason for doing this
K an haha wo i ha-uliñhogid g e-ṣoṣoiga	But now your horses should rest
Kut o i em-wa:pagidahi	You will be wakened
Mat hekid g taṣ ab abṣ o cem sikol i me:."	When the sun is about to rise."

Am hebai ha'i wo na:d
Ṣon am am e-wehemadc o wo:piwa
K am hu waṣ o i wo'iyo
T hegam am o daḍiya hegam s-u:gcu'u
We:skij at am o dada
Am na:dajid
Heg we:gaj am o daḍage, o a'agad ha'icu.

Someplace some of them will make a fire
At its base they will gather and lie
That is where they will bed down
But the leaders will stay up
They have all arrived
They will make a fire
They will sit around it and discuss something.

Am hekid am b i cei hegai t-u:gcu'u
"Pegi, k oi am has o i e-ju:"
K am a ha'ap hi o ho-we:m ñeñok.

When our leader will speak
"Well, there is something to do"
Then he will hold discussions.

Ñe:, t am o hi: g ak ciñk ha-u:gcu'uga
Am ep hi o na:dk
Am ep hi o ho-je:ñig
Matp he'ekiac am wuḍ ep hi i ha-u:gcudahim
T g wi:piop an abṣ o wo:pia.

The Ak Chin leader will also go
He will also make a fire
And will also hold a meeting
With as many as are leaders
But the boys will merely sleep.

I:dam hab a masma sil nagia
Hegam am wo daḍiya
Matp heḍai wuḍ o i ha-u:gcu'u
A:ngam hab a masma
Pegi, t hegam hia ep wo daḍiya heg e:p.

These from Sil Nagia
Will also be sitting up
If they are leaders
Anegam [group] is the same
Well, they will also be sitting up.

Ñe: mo i:ya wuḍ t-taccui
I:dam o ho-ga:g g sisiakam
Mat hegam o kokda.

Look, this was our desire
That they would seek out the heroes
To do the killing.

Hemako om i wu:ṣ
Pegi, t ab ha-ma:g aki ciñ
T hegam am i ep wu:ṣad hegai
Heu'u, i:dam hik sil nagia
Pegi, t ab i wu:ṣadk ab hema we:nad
Pegi, b a masma hab cu'ig hegai.

One [candidate] will come out
Well, and they give it to Ak Chin
They have to pick another one
Yes, and these from Sil Nagia
Well, they may pick one to be with him
Well, that is how it is.

Masma hab o ju:
Mat o ṣa p i nako i:dam go'olkol ki:dag
B hema o ho-ma:
O ṣa go:ko pi e-na:ko i:dam ki:kam.

But it may happen
That the different villages don't succeed
To appoint somebody
Or they can't get two from these groups.

Pegi, k t hab masma am o hi:
B o wa masma hab o o-ju:
Matp am hema pi e:p
Kutp i: hasko hema wo bei e:p.

Well, that's how it goes
It happens that way
That they can't get another
Then from somewhere else around here they get him.

B o wa masma hab cu'ig i:da
S-ta-e:bidaṃa has s-ta:hadag
"Pi o t-na:ko i:ya

That's how this is
It feels dangerous to them
"We can't do it [find a candidate] from here

I:ya wuḍ t-ki:dag
Mac wuḍ taccuikam
Pi o t-na:ko
Pi ap ta:had
I:dam o o-na:ko mo go'olkol ki:dag ab
Hegam o bei mas hascu am b i cu'ig."

This is our life
We like it
So we can't do it
It's too bad
But the other villages can do it
They can get the one who will be that."

B o wa masma hab cu'ig hegai
Ñe:, k t oiya hab e-ju:
Mat hab masma am o ho-ma: e:p
Pegi, t i o e-na:to hegam
Mo hab ḥia cem masma hab cu'ig
Mañ ab ep ñeid hegai.

That's how this is
Look, and then it happens
That they give it to another place
Well, and that place can do it
Yes it was like this
When I saw it [a Santa Rosa man was selected].

I ton g ma:sidag
T hi s-ho:ho'id
Pegi, k t ha-kokda hegai.

The dawn shines
They like it
Well, and they kill them.

Pegi, t am hema wo mel hegai
K am o a:g
"Meḍk am i ha-a:gidahim
Kut ab o i hemapa
I at hu wa ap'et."

Well, someone will run
He will tell [someone else]
"Run and tell them [back at the camp]
So they will gather up
It's all right now."

An aha wa meḍk
T we:sij gḍ hu wo i hemapa
At am o gegokia hegam sisiakam.

So he will run
Everyone will gather back there
Where they will stand up the heroes.

Heki hu o na:tokjid ha'icu hegai ha-u:gcu'u
We:s ha'icu o na:to am ha-we:hejeḍ
S-toha ikus
B a masma mo g *scarf*
Mo o-na:to.

Already their leader will have something ready for them
He will have everything ready for them
A white cloth
Like a scarf
Will be ready.

U:s hikomiyo
K wuḍ o hegaikad
Mas wuḍ ha-keskuḍ hegai
T heki hu o na:to.

A cut stick
Will be used for something
That is their hair tyer
And it will be ready.

Ñe:, t hekid am o i e-na:to hegai
Pegi, k am o him
K am o ho-u'apa hegam.

Look, and when they are ready
Well, he will go
And bring them [heroes].

Am o ha'i gegoho go:k hegam
Mo ḍ ha-ñu:kudam
T hegam o ho-ñu:kud.

Two others will be standing by
Who are their caretakers [for the heroes]
And they will take care of them.

T hegam in hu hia wo:pod hegam

Those [who killed nothing] will be running around

T hegam gḍ hu hi wuḍ a'i hegaikad
Mat g am o i cegia hegai.

And those [heroes] will be back there
Who were in the fighting.

Hekid o i e-na:tok
T ab o ho-ui hegam
Mo ho-u'uk
Gm hu ho-cu:cia.

When it is ready
They will bring them [heroes]
Will carry them
Will stand them there.

Huḍuñ wui wo cu:cia
Am aha wa hema wo a:gi
"Meḍk ab i ha-waid
Mat o wa'i i ap'et hegai"
Ñe:, t am aha wo ho-wai
T am aha wo i wuwhas hegai
K g hekaj o si'iṣ hegai
An o ho-gewṣ hab masma mo g nawaho

Towards the west they will stand them
Then someone will say
"Run over and call them
Since now it is time"
Look, and then they will call them
They will take out the things
With which to fasten [their hair]
They will hold it down like a Navaho [hairdo]

K wuḍ hegai mas wuḍ keskuḍ.

That is what the hair tyer is for.

C hegai masma mo g kuipad matsig

And that which is like the hook on a cactus picking pole

Masma wo hiwṣa g ṣegai

Which is made by scraping a greasewood stick

Im o wa:k i:ma
T heg wuḍ o ho-hu:ckad hegai.

It is put in here [into the hair bun]
And serves as their finger nail.

Am o ho-a:g hegam
"Pi ab hu wo hukṣa"
Wo cegitokc g an o bei hegai

They will tell them
"Never scratch yourself"
They will remember and will take that [scratcher]

Wo hekaj hegai.

And use it.

Hekid an o i ha'as e-hukṣañ
K an a ab o wa:k e:p
Hekid hasko s-mohogid
Wuḍ a'i hegai.

Whenever they finish their scratching
They will put it back in
Until something itches again
That's the way that is.

Pegi, k am aha wa wo ho-a:gi hegai hegam

Well, and then they will speak

Mat in o oiyopo
T hab o cei
"Pegi, k i: o gegokia i:dam

Those who are going about there
And they will say
"Well, here they stand

Mat t-we: hejeḍ gegokia
We: s o ḍ t-s-ap'ed
We: s t-we: hejeḍ gekokia
Pegi, k i: da cikp i: da
K wuḍ si ha'icu
Kuc si has e-elid hegai
Si ha'icu am t-we: hejeḍ
Mat heg i hab ju: g t-jeweḍga
We: s t-jeweḍga we: hejeḍ
We: sko om i hab cu'ig i: da
Mac he'ekiapaj ab t-jeweḍga ab i ha'icug hegai.

They stand here for us
Everything is for our good
As they stand for all of us
Well, and this was work
It is really something
We respect it
It is really something to us
That this was done for our land
For all of our land
For every place
For as many places as we have as our land.

C wuḍ i: dam
Mat i: dam ab t-we: hejeḍ gegokia
Cecoj e-a'aga am gegokia ab t-we: hejeḍ
Pi has o ṣa'i elidadad ha'icu
Am t-we: hejeḍ gegokia
We: sij wuḍ t-ap'edag hegai
Kutp pi heḍai im hu hab o kaij."

And it is these [heroes]
These who are standing for us
They are standing for manhood for us
They don't care for anything
As they stand for us
It is for all of our good
And nobody will say anything [bad]."

Hema am o ñiokad
C am hebai wo i ku: gi
K am hema ep wo ke: kiwa
Am b o cei
"Mo om a woho
Mo ḍ i: da mac i: da ga: gkhim
I: da c g hekaj i himcud t-ki: dagga, t-jeweḍga"
Heg ep wo ñio
Matp hema has i masma wo s-e-amicud
Id oidk o ñio
K o ce: mo'o.

One of them will be talking
And sometime he'll finish
Then another one will stand up
He will say
"It's true
That it's this that we were seeking
It's this that will drive our society and our land"
Another one will say it
If that is what he understands
So he will continue to speak
And he will finish.

T am o wa gegokc wo kaihim
B o s-amicud
g t-i: bdag o meḍdad
No pi am wuḍ a si ha'icu.

They [heroes] stand there listening
They understand it
Their hearts are running
Because it is a very big thing.

Pegi ñe:, t amjeḍ am ha'ap o o-cei
Wo o-ñiok
"Hemu idañ hia s-ap'e
Mat am a s-ap ju: hegai
Mo ha'icu hab wuḍ t-taccuidag
We: s t-ki: dag s-ap ju:.

Well look, then it will be said like this
Someone will speak
"Now it's fine
It has been done well
According to our desires
Our whole society has done well.

Hemu i: ya na: tok
O hia pi has cu'ig

Now it's finished
There is nothing to it

I ho-ma: g e-nowi
Kut i o ho-dagito."

So give them your hands
And let them go."

Ñe:, k ab aha wa i hi:
Heg at t-nowi bebbe
Ñe:, b o cei g t-u:gcu'u
"Heg o ma: g e-gewkdag
Mo ḍ si ha'icu
S-ap amt gewito ha'icu am eḍa."

Look, and then they start
They take our hands
Look, and our leader says
"They will give their strength
Which is really something
You have won it well in that [war]."

O ho-ma: g e-hajuñ e-nowi
"T ab em-ab o gewkdag"
Ñe:, k ab t-we:sij ab t-nowi bebbe
Ab t-i:m
He'es am i ñiokimc ab i ñiokim
Pegi, i at hab masma hab e-ju: k e-ju: k e-ju:.

They give their relatives their hands
"This will make you strong"
Look, and they all take our hands
They state their kinship to us
They talk and talk
Well, and that's the way it happens here.

Hekid am o i ha'asa hegai
Ñe:, k am aha wo ha'i ha-a:g hegam go:k

When they quit that
Look, then they will tell two of them

"Napt o me:
o ho-kailig g hemajkam."

"Won't you run
To notify the people [at home]."

Pi heḍai ma:c hegam
Mas heḍai hu wuḍ o i hegaikad g siakam
Heḍai hu wuḍ o i ce:gigc o o-uapa
Pi heḍai ma:c.

None of them know
Who will be the heroes
Whose name will be brought
None of them know.

"Ñe:, mat hemu wo wo:p"
T eḍa ab o i ma:si
Ñe: at o wo:p.

"Look, now they will run"
Yet it is dawn
Look, and they run.

Hema e-ga:t o uad
T hema o s-ba'iyudkam
Mat s-kaidam o hihin
Pegi, k o wo:p amai
O wo:p k o wo:p
K hekid g gm hu o i wo'i
Mat am o i wa:p ki:himc eḍ
K o gatwui
Gi'iko gatwi
Pegi, t o ha-wu:pa g hemajkam.

One of them carries a gun
One has a loud throat
So he can yell plainly
Well, and they run there
Run and run
And when they arrive
When they enter the village
He will shoot
Four times shoot
Well, that is to wake up the people.

T am aha wo hihin hegai
Kaidam o hihin
Mas hema o d s-ba'iyudkam
K am o hihin

Then the other one will yell
Loudly he yells
The one with the good throat
He will yell

Am o a:
"Ka:los, ka:los at ha-mua
Amant, aman at ha-mua"
T we:sij o i wu:pa g hemajkam.

He will say
"Carlos, Carlos killed them
Armando, Armando killed them"
All the people will be awakened.

B o wa masma hab o a ju: ga hu amjeḍ, a:ngam

They do the same over at Anegam

O ho-ma: g ha-cecegid
We:sko ot hab a:g
Hab masma o s-e-mai.

They give them the names
They tell it every place.
Thus they will know.

Pegi, t am o si e-mai hegam
T hegam gm hu wo i wo:p
Ab u:hum o i wo:p hegam
Mat am ha-kailig
U:hum o himk
Ga hu wo ho-nam mat ab o i hihimad.

Well, and then they will really know
So those will run off
They will run back again
Who notified them
Back they go
And there they will meet those who are coming [war party].

T hab o o-ju:
Eḍa am o i ceṣ g taṣ
A'aijeḍ o i i-hemapa g hemajkam
S-masma o i hi: g ku:bs ga hu amjed
T heki hu o hemapa g o'odham
Pegi ñe:, k amjed hab o o-ju:
T heḍai wuḍ o i we:peg

It will happen
Yet the sun is just rising
The people will gather from all over
Their dust can be seen from back there
They will have gathered
Well look, and then it will happen
Whoever [of the war party] is the first to arrive

T o ṣa mel' gḍ hu
Gi'iko on i da'ibij anai

He will run over there
Four times he will circle [the gathered people]

K an o dagito g e-ṣoiga.

Then will get off his horse.

Eḍa am heki hu kekiwa g keli o'odham
Bek g e-ṣawkud
K o ho-ñei g li:mhu
Gan hu wo gegokia we:maj
T hegam o wo'i
Matp hekid o i hihimk we:sij o gegokia
T hekid g gm hu wo i himad hegam
I ñeñopa g o'oki
Ha-ṣagid o i wa:
Ñe:, k t o hi: g li:mhu ñe'i.

By then an old man will be standing
He has brought his rattle
And will sing the *li: mhu* [songs]
They will be standing with him
They will arrive
When they have all come they will stand
And when they are about ready to leave
Old women will come out
And will enter between them
Look, and the *li: mhu* songs will continue.

Hema wuḍ o si heki hu hemajkam
Kut eḍa o uad g u:s
Gn hu o nagia g ikus wi:dagi
Matp wuḍ o:b ha-eñiga.

Someone will be a very old person
But she will take the stick
Where the torn rag hangs
Which is the enemy's property.

An o bekk an o uad	He [leader] will take it and carry it
K am o kei amai je:gs eḍa	And will stand it on the cleared ground
O kei hegai ha-u:gcu'u	The leader will stand it there
Pegi, t heḍai am o i s-amicud	Well, and whoever will know how
O'oks	Of the old ladies
Wo meḍk am o bei hegai	Will run and take it
K am o kekiwa	Will stand holding it
Wo ñei hegai	Will sing
Wo ge:g ha'icu	Will win something
Hema hascu o i eḍagidc am o o-ge:gc	If someone has something and it will be won
B o o-juñhimk juñhim	They will do it and do it
Ñe:, t am u:hum ep o ma: hegai	Look, and then she will give it back
Mo heḍai wuḍ i eñiga	To whoever is the owner
T am o u:pam kei e:p.	And he will stand it up again.
Ñe:, k an hu waha wo ke:kia	Look, and then he will stand holding it
K o o-li:mhu k e-li:mhu	They will *li:mhu* and *li:mhu*
O huḍ g taṣ	The sun sets
Eḍa gḍ hu wo daḍekad	Yet they [heroes] will be sitting off someplace
C si wa ha-ka:kad.	And will certainly be hearing them.
Ñe:, ñ-eda a:ñi go:ko ho-ñeid	Look, at that time I had seen it twice [before]
C abṣ am b i ha-elid	And thought
Mo hab masma hab e-ju:	That it would be like that [for me again]
Eḍa ñ-gḍ hu ha'icug	Yet now I was over there [as a hero]
Ñe:, amjeḍ hab a ṣ masma am ka:.	Look, and from there all one can do is hear.
Ñe:, t am hab e-ju:	Look, then it happens
Hekid am o i huhug	When they will stop
T am aha wo ho-a:g	And he [leader] will tell them [celebrators]
Mat am a s-ap'et	That it is all right
"Mampt am o hihi	"You can go
Mo o-uliñhogid	Take a rest
I: g kawhi:	Drink coffee
E-gegos	Eat
Mat hekid o i huḍuñ	Until it is night
Mampt i wo dada e:p."	Then you will arrive back here again."
Ñe:, t eḍa gam hu i pi has cei	Look, then over there there was no sound
T eḍa a:cim i hu wo daḍakad	Where we were sitting
K am o i huḍ	And it was sunset
Hab o ju:	Then it happens
Mat am o u'apa t-gegosig	That he [caretaker] will bring our food

Ab o i dahiwa
K i ha'icu wo t-a:gi
K o him mo him k o him.

He will sit down
He will tell us something
And go on and on and on.

Ñe:, gm hu wo ṣa'i s-cuk
T o ṣonwa g ñe'i
Hua wo ṣonwa
Ha-ñe'icul
Hihink i o meḍdad
S am o taṣokad mo has masma hab
e-wua.

Look, and then it was very dark
The songs start
The basket [scraping] starts
They sing for it
Shouts are running
And it is very clear what they are doing.

Kant am abṣ ka:kad g ñe'i
Ñe:, ṣ hab a a cem an daḍiwa
T hekid o ku:gt hegai ñe'i
Matp hekid o eḍa hugkam s-cuhugkam
Gam hu a'ai wo hihim
T eḍa a:cim wo daḍakad
T am aha wo wo:piwa.

I could just hear the songs
Look, but I was sitting there
And when the songs stopped
When the night was halfway through
Then they went their various ways
Yet we remained sitting there
And then we might lie down.

Ha'ap a'i s-hu:g
Mant o kupal wo'ia
C heg hab a ep o o-ju:

The only way to keep warm
Was for me to lay on my stomach
And he [the other hero] did the same
thing

Ñe:, t am o wo:piwa
Hi wa t-je:ñgid t-we:m
Ñe:, t am hebai wa aha wa i ko:k.

Look, and we lay there
Of course we talked to each other
Look, and sometimes we slept.

Eḍa ṣa'i pi t-abam
G hewel meliuw
S o wa t-ce'ehic hegai
S wi'ickwa
Ñ hab a:gid hegai ñ-nawoj
"Pi g has ṣa'i e-ta:tk i:da
Att o nakokad i:da
Id am t hekaj am t-dagito
Kutt wuḍ o cecojc o nako
Pi has o ṣa'i e-ta:tkad."

But it was our bad luck
The wind started to blow
We covered ourselves up
It blew them off
I said to my friend
"Don't feel that
We will stand it
This is why they left us here
And we are men and can stand it
So don't be feeling anything."

Ñe: k am hebai waha wa i ko:k
T abṣ hab a ha wo ṣa al has o i e-ju:
g ma:sidag

Look, and sometime we slept
But it was almost morning

T o ji:wia hegai
"Oig o wa:pag
K as o daḍakad"
Kutt a wa:pagk ep daḍa
Ñe:, t am ep wo t-je:ñgi e:p

He [caretaker] will come
"Go ahead and get up
Be sitting"
And so we got up and sat
Look, and he has another meeting
with us

"Hia e-ju: hia
T o hia e-hemapadk am b hia e-ju:

"Of course it will happen
Of course they [celebrators] will gather
and do it

S-ap hab cu'ig
Hab a pi has o ṣa'i e-ta:tk
Pi it has o ṣa'i em-ju:.

That's good
But you won't feel anything
They won't trouble you.

Mapt abṣ o ba'iwuc i:da ha'icu na:nko
ta:hadkam

You will pass through this kind of feeling

Im at hu ha'ap hu im-wañim hegai
Kut wuḍ o hegai
Im hu ha'ap hihim
Bṣ o pi cegito hegai
Mo hascu hab i i-wua.

It could lead you away
But it is that [sorrow]
It goes off someplace
Just don't think about it
Whatever happens.

S-he:ki g hemajkam
Hab a em-amjeḍ
Map hemu ia daha
Heg amjeḍ s-he:ki g hemajkam
Wuḍ hegai mampt pi has ṣa'i e-ta:tk."

The people are happy
It's due to you
You who sit here
That's what makes the people happy
That's what you must not feel."

Ñe:, g amjeḍ o ñio k o ñio k o ñio
K amjeḍ o hi:
Am o si ma:si
T o daḍiwakad hegai
Ñe: k oiya k am b aha wa cei
"Mampt aha wa ep wo i wo:piya
K am abṣ al ha'as o i i-uliñhogi"
Ñe:, ant am aha wo ku'ukpal i wo:piwa
K am o him
Ṣa'i ha'as t ep wo ji:wia k o u'ad g t-bi:

Look, then he talks and talks and talks
Then he goes
It is dawn
They will be sitting
Look, then he will say
"Now you can lay down
It is time to rest for a while"
Look, and I lay down
And he goes
After a while he returns again with our
serving

T hascu al i t-ma: hegai
"Oig o wa:pagk o dadiwa
O hug hegai"
K am o i wa:pag
K am ep o dadiwa
Ep wo t-ma: hegai.

Whatever he gives to us [to eat]
"Go ahead and wake up and sit
Eat this"
And we get up
We sit again
And again he gives it to us.

Ñe:, si'ali am o wa ji:wia
Am o t-wa:pag hegai
Ñe: gm hu ep wo him
T hekid am o i e-a'ahe hegai
T ep wo i t-uliñhogid.

Look, in the morning he comes
He gets us up
Look, and he goes back again
Then it's time
We rest again.

Kut am ep wo ji:wia
"Oig o wa:pag hegai"
T ep o i wa:pag
K am ep wo daḍiwa.

And he comes again
"Go ahead and get up"
We get up again
We sit up again.

Ñe:, k hab o i huḍ
K am ep wo ji:wia e:p
Ep wo w-hemapak ep ṣonc g ñe'i

Gamai hu g s-he:kigkam o i wu:ṣañ hegai
Ha-ce'idag am ep wo kaidag.

Look, and it is sunset
He arrives again
Also the people are gathering and the singing starts
Away off there the happiness comes out

Their expressions sound again.

T am o wa daḍakad
Gi'ik s-cuhugamc gi'ik taṣ
D o i hetaṣp taskaj
Matt o i wuwha gm hu.

We will be sitting
Four days and four nights
It is on the fifth day
That we get out from there.

Ñe: k am hia ha-a:gid hia hegam

Mac hebai dada
Mat pi am hu wo ṣa'i dada
Pi am hu wo ho-kuḍutad hegai
S-ta wa i e:bidam hegai.

Look, and of course they tell them [celebrators]
That we are arriving someplace
That they shouldn't go there
They won't bother it [us]
It is dangerous.

Ñe:, t o wa am ia a'ahim
Mat gm hu hab o e-ju: g wulida
In g ha-himaj g ha-ñiok
S-kaidam b o kaij
"Pi g am hu ha'ap o hihim
Amai ṣ o daḍiwa amai hegam."

Look, it's getting close to the time
When there will be the tying
Off there goes their talking
Loudly they say
"Don't go over that way
That is where they are sitting."

A:cim o daḍakad
Am aha wa ji:wia hegai t-u:gcu'u
Am b aha kaij
"Pegi oig
Na'as hemu am a a'ahe hegai."

We will be sitting there
Then will arrive our leader
He will say
"Well go ahead
Apparently the time has come."

Ga hu amjeḍ ab i i-hemapa
E ge kakambo g hemajkam
Anai man jegc eḍ
Eḍa s-t-ma:cim
Matt hekid o i wuwha
K amjeḍ kakambo.

Off there they are gathering
The people are setting up camp
Off on open ground
Because they know about us
When we will come out
Therefore they make camp.

Hihiḍodk am hu i e-gegos
Haha wa ep o melc g s-he:kig
Ñe:, t am aha wa wuwha.

They cook and later eat
Happiness passes through them
Look, and then we are released.

Gam hu wa i juñhim hegai
Mat i t-wuwha
Am hi: hegai t-u:gcu'u
Ñ-am oidc him
K ab ñ-oid hegai.

It was almost sunset
When they released us
Our leader went over there
I followed him
And the other one [hero] followed me.

Kaij, "Pi ipt an hu wo ṣa'i ha-ñenhogkad
Mapt o wa'i ñiacogkad i:ya
Hegam at hab hi wa m-ñeidad"
Ñe:, t amjeḍ am hihim
Hemajkam ha-babṣo hihim
Gḍ hu ai amai
Mo om we:c g ku'agi
Am ha-cu:cia g u'us
Go:k wuḍ hegai
K am ep ge wa:pagt e:p
T g eḍa am o dadiwa.

He said, "Don't be looking around
Just look right here [in front]
Those can be looking at you"
Look, and they go
In front of the people they go
Arrive over there
Where the firewood lays
They have set up posts
Two of them
They have also dug holes
In them they [heroes] sit.

T-daḍṣ amai
Am-ui g t-wopnam
Heg ab an ha-nangia.

They sit us there
They take our hats
They hang them on them [posts]

Ñe: t oi am dadaiya
I ha'as hu'i am ha-a:gahim hegam
Matṣ hegam wuḍ t-ñe'icul hegam.

Look, and they have sat down
In a little while they will be singing
Whoever will sing for us.

O hema wo a:
"Oig am i himk i hu dahiwa"
S-ma:c mo eḍa s-ma:c hegai ñeñe'i
T in o dahiwa
Gn hu i hugkam o daha
K i:da ab a hebai ab daicug hegai
Mo ha'icu ṣ hab wuḍ kapaḍwa.

They will tell one of them
"Come over and sit down"
They know who knows the songs
They sit beside him [main singer]
For some distance in a line they sit
And this one sits waiting
Who is the war dancer.

K g o bei g kawaḍ
Heg am nagiakc hegai t-da:m hegai
Pegi, t am heki hu hema wo a: hegai
"A:ñi, nt o bei hegai"
s-e-da'iud hegai
s-e-da'a hegai.

He will get the shield
It hangs above us
Well, somebody will have said
"I, I'll get it"
He would like to keep others from it
He's stingy about it.

Hema hab o cei
"A:ñi, nt o bei we:peg"
Mo ṣa s-ap'e
Am o nagia
T am aha wa hema ep o cem ji:wia
Heki at hu bei hegai
Ñe:, t g am o bei.

Someone will say
"I, I'll get it first"
That's fine
There it hangs
Then someone else will come up
But it has already been taken
Look, the first one got it.

Ñe:, k am aha wa hekid o i e-na.to
Am o ṣonwa hegai
Am o nai gḍ hu
T o mei
B o ton hegai

Look, then when it is ready
They will start
They will make a fire there
It will burn
It will shine

Ñe:, t i aha wa da'iwuṣ hegai
Mat o bei g kawaḍ
T eḍa o ṣonc i:da ñe'i.

Look, then he [war dancer] springs out
Who will take the shield
Then the singing begins.

Ñe:, t i aha wo bei hegai
K amjeḍ am o meḍ gḍ hu
Eḍa am o tondadc o s-ma:skad
Amjeḍ o dadahi, dadahi
Gḍ hu o wa: gḍ hu amai
Gḍ hu tai we:gaj
Has masma o i s-e-ma:c
Eḍa wuḍ keli o'odham
S-ma:c mat has masma na:nko masma keihina.

Look, then he gets it
He runs from there
Where it is shining and visible
Then he jumps and jumps
He will go in back there
Behind the fire
In whatever manner he knows
Although he is an old man
He knows many ways to dance.

Ñe:, t g oidk hema hab o o-elidad g oks, uwi
Mat hascu an o i bei
T-wonam, ha'icu t-eniga
O bekk oidk keihi
An hab o wa juñhim.

Look, meanwhile an old lady or woman may think
That she will get something
Our hat, something of our property
She gets it and dances with it
She will be doing this.

Ñe:, k am ep o o-ju:
Ñe:, hab o o-ju: cuhug oid
Eḍa mu'ic hegai.

Look, and another will do it
Look, they do it all night
Since they are many.

Go:k am o ho-a:
K hab aha wo ma: hegai
Mat in hu hugid an daha
Am o ho-a: hegai go:k.

Two songs will be sung
Then he gives it [right to sing] to him
Who sits beside him [first singer]
He will sing two.

K am hekid am o i ku:gi hegai
B aha wa ji:wia
B aha wa t-wusot
T-wusotk am o t-ñe'ic
K am o t-wusot
Ñe:, k im hu wo hi: hegai
Pegi, t ab o ma: hegai.

When he stops
He comes up
He blows on us
Blows on us and sings to us
And he blows on us
Look, then he goes back [to sit down]
Well, and gives it to the next [singer].

T am aha ep hi o ho-a: e:p go:k
K hekid am o i ku:gi hegai go:k
K am ep wo ji:wia
K am ep wo t-wuso e:p
Pegi, k im hu wo hi:.

He will sing two more [songs]
When he finishes the two
Then he will come
He will also blow on us
Well, then he goes back.

Ep wo ma: hegai
Mat an ep wo da:kad
T eḍa hab t-ju:

He gives it to another
Who sits beside him
But it happens to us

Matt o gewko
T am o dada hegam
B aha wo i ju: k ab o t-ui
Mo i t-wuwhasid
T am o gegokia
Ha'as am o i gegok
T eḍa wo je:j hegam
Ep o t-daḍṣp e:p
K am ep wo daḍiwa
Eḍa o ha'asa je:je.

That we get tired
So they come
They grab us
They pull us out [of the holes]
They stand us
They stand us for a while
While they smoke
Then they set us back again
We are seated again
When the smoking is finished.

T g am ep wo ṣonc e:p go:k ne'i
T am ep wo t-wuso
T am ep wo ha-a:gi
"Matto je:j"
Pegi, t am ep wo i t-wuwha
Ñe:, b masma am b o wa ju:.

They begin two more songs
They blow on us again
Again they say
"Let's smoke"
Well, and they take us out again
Look, that's how it is done.

T hekid am o i ku:g
T am aha wo a:gi hegam
Aki ciñ, a:ngam, sil nagiak i:ya

When they finish [the war dancing]
They tell those
From Ak Chin, Anegam, Sil Nagia, and here

P heḍai am hab o i e-elid
C o s-wuam g hua
K o ho-ñe'ic hegai
Ñe:, t am aha hejel o o-na:ko
Gḍ hu o wua i:dam g ñe'i
Keihina ñe'i.

Whoever will wish
To take the basket
And sing [other kinds of songs] for them
Look, they do it on their own
Off someplace they put the songs
Keihina songs.

Hegam aki ciñ, sil nagia, a:ngam hasko om wua
B o masma wui me: g hemajkam
Keihina ñe'i
Hasko om o keihi
C hasko e:p
C hasko e:p b i masma hab o o-ju:
K o him.

Those from Ak Chin, Sil Nagia, and Anegam do it someplace
People run there
Keihina songs
Keihina dancing at one place
And another place [among the camps]
And at still another place thus they do it
And it goes.

Ñe:, t eḍa g am a s-amicud
Mat hekid o i huhug hegam
Mat am a ñe'ic
Pegi, t am aha wa ji:wia
K am aha wa t-a:g hegai
"Hemu am a we:s ce:mo'o"
B aha wo cu'ig matt am aha wo waccui.

Look, but they know
When those stop
Who are singing
Well, then they will arrive
And tell us
"Now everything is complete"
So it is that they will wash us.

Gḍ hu wo dai g ha'a
Ṣu:dagi am ṣu:dag

They will set down an olla
Full of water

K hemu ha'a k ṣa'i s-he:pid

It's a new olla that makes the water very cold

Eḍa ab i ma:si gḍ hu wuḍ i *November*
S-he:pid.

Yet it is dawn in November
Cold.

Ñe:, t eḍa am o daḍiwa
Am aha wa i t-e'eñigadipi'o
T heg ab wo ke:kia g keli o'odham
Wasibk tua hegai s-he:p ṣu:dagi
Ñe:, k am o ñio
Am aha wo wasib
Masma am o iawa t-mo'o da:m hegai s-he:p ṣu:dagi
Amjeḍ o ñio k o ñio k o ñio
S g oidam o s-he:p.

Look, they sit down
Then we take off our clothes
An old man stands up
He dips some of the cold water
Look, he talks ['cure speech']
Then he dips it
Then he pours it on our heads

Afterwards he talks and talks and talks
Meanwhile it is cold.

Gm hu wo ku:g hegai
Ñe:, t i ab ep ju:
K am ep wasib
T am ep t-iawa
Oidk ab me: g s-he:p ṣu:dagi
Eḍa ab i ma:si
Ep ñio k ñio.

Finally he will finish
Look, and they do it again
They dip it again
And pour it on us
The cold water runs along
Yet it is dawn
Again he talks and talks.

Ñe:, mo ḍ a'i go:k
Ñe:, k wuḍ i go:k e:p
T am ep iawa e:p hegai
K am ep ñio e:p
Ñio k ñio
He'es i taṣ am gegok
B aha kaij, "Do:ho'i"
B at aha wa hema a:
"Oig o o-wapkwan"
Am aha wa bṣ ce: hegai
Ñe:, ṣ wasibc ab si iawa

Look, those are only two
Look, and there are two more
Again they pour it
Again they talk
And talk and talk
We stayed standing
Finally he said, "Done"
Then someone said
"Go and wash yourselves"
There they stood it [olla]
Look, we dipped it and really poured it on

No pi hab kaij hegai
"Pi has ṣa'i elidad
D am p ṣ si cioj hegai
Mat heg hekaj wuḍ o si cecojkad."

Because they had said
"Don't think about it
This is for a man
To be real men."

Ṣ am hewet
Mu'i ñiok t-mai
S-ap e-kaij
Ñe:, k oiya t-ma: g *towels* hekaj dagkwa

Wind blew
They gave us many speeches
It sounded nice
Look, then they gave us towels to wipe ourselves

Am aha t-ma: g t-eñiga
Am aha hab kaij
"Pegi, oig o am a ṣ haha e-juñ hegai."

Next they gave us our clothes
And said
"Well, go and do what you want."

Ñe:, b wa:m heg am me:k hi:	Look, he [the other hero] had far to go
Gam i hu aki ciñ wui	Far to Ak Chin
I wañmeḍk hab kaij	They led him and said
"Pegi oig hi: matt o hihi"	"All right, let's go"
Ñe:, im hu ab hihi	Look, and they went
Eḍa im abṣ k ia kaidag, na:nko kaidaghim	Still there were sounds, many sounds
He:kigculid.	Of happiness.
Ñe: c hema hia uacug g ṣondal li:wa	Look, and someone took his soldier jacket
Heg ab wua	He put it on
Ba wa kaij	And said
"Pegi, nt hi wo hi:"	"Well, I'll be going"
"Oig ṣa'ali"	"Go ahead"
T-nowi bebbe	He shook our hands
"Mo wa s-ap'e	"This is fine
Hemu apt g hu wo ji:wia	You'll soon be there
Map a ka: mo has kaij g hemajkam	As you've heard the people say
Mo heg apt o hekaj	Where you'll use this
Hemu apt g hu wo ji:wia"	You'll soon be there"
K a:cim ia ha ep dada.	And we, too, soon arrived [at home].

This war campaign was in November, consistent with what we said about the preferred time for making war. Two questions arise: How much control did Papagos have over making war in old times, and was all of their warfare cast in the form of the *gidahim*? It is felt that Papagos had considerable control over their warring subsequent to the 1850s, for they were allies of the U.S. Army. Their situation was different from the enemies they fought against, mostly Apaches and Yavapais (both called *o:b*, 'enemy', in Papago), because the Papagos were encouraged to keep guns and horses and their enemies were not. They were paid wages when they worked as scouts or soldiers. Roughly the same was true during the Spanish and Mexican periods. Thus for nearly three hundred years the Papagos were allied, consciously or not, with the winning side in European-Indian conflicts in their territory. This may have affected their outlook or the conditions under which they fought. We cannot show it, however. There is not a word about guns or horses in the war speeches. They sound as if Europeans did not exist.

Gidahim designates a planned expedition into enemy territory. Obviously that is only half of the war story. Papagos were sometimes attacked and forced to fight without planning. No doubt many of their planned raids were also in response to previous attacks. There should have been a point at which a response was so immediate that it was not a question of a planned war campaign, but of hot pursuit. We don't know how often that point was crossed. All we feel safe in saying is that *gidahim* was the preferred way for Papagos to go to war, in the winter, with plenty of time for planning, and usually, as we will see, in search of an enemy whose exact location was not known. They preferred to go hunting for enemies in much the same way as they went hunting for deer.

A final explanation is needed on the degree that all Papago warfare was subsumed under the *gidahim*. The only enemies in this kind of war were Indians. During the 20th century Papagos have fought for the United States against Germans, Italians, Japanese, North Koreans, Chinese, and Vietnamese but the customs and restrictions of *gidahim* do not apply to those enemies. The returned soldiers are not *sisiakam*. Thus the end of real Papago *gidahim* (as opposed to raids against 'straw enemies') was at the end of the American pacification of the Arizona frontier.

The following is a phase by phase account of the *gidahim*, with speeches, as it was described to Ruth Underhill and Marie Gunst in the late 1920s and early 1930s, and described by Baptisto Lopez, above. Underhill's full discussion is contained in *Papago Indian Religion* (1946:165-210) and *Social Organization of the Papago Indians* (1939:128-138). The account by Gunst is in an unpublished Masters' Thesis written for the University of Arizona in 1929. All these descriptions pertain primarily to Santa Rosa and its neighboring villages, Ak Chin, Anegam, and Ge Aji.

PREPARATIONS

These commenced with a speech. One of the reasons why the war campaign stands as such a long ritual is that it involved oratory from beginning to end. There are more orations for this rite than for any other. The opening speech refers to a very well known episode in the Papago creation story, the death and revival of a god named *I'itoi* (also called *Si:s Ma:kai*, 'Elder Brother Medicine Man'). Briefly the story is this. After driving the ancestors of the Papagos into the underworld by causing a flood, I'itoi made a new race who tried to kill him. He died and came back to life—an event narrated in the preface of the speech below. Then he journeyed eastward, ascended into the sky where the sun rises, followed its path through the sky, and descended into the underworld where the sun sets. There he met the Papagos and recruited them as an army against the people who had killed them. He led the Papagos back to earth, they defeated his enemies, and the Papagos settled in their present villages.

The speech leaves I'itoi making war alone against some objects he encountered on the road to the underworld. It does not finish the story of his reunion with the Papagos in the underworld and the subsequent emergence of the tribe.[1]

All accounts of the preparations stress that a proper *gidahim* involved more than one village. Giving the I'itoi speech was the official means for one village to notify another that a raid was upcoming, just as giving the 'running' speech was the official way to notify a village that a 'sit and drink' would be held. Of course there would be informal communications as well. These, for warfare, are stressed in Mr. Lopez' account. He does not mention the I'itoi speech at all and generally does not stress the role of oratory in the war campaign. This is not because oratory was not used in his experience, but because he has left that task for the writing of this commentary.

[1]Other versions of the speech do that and may be consulted in *Pima-Papago Ritual Oratory* by Bahr, 1975.

I'ITOI SPEECH

Juan Gregorio, Santa Rosa

Ha'ap 'ant a wa'i do:da, si:s ma:kai, cu:iko hejel wua, ka'am ka:ckahim da:am gi'ik si'alim e-ce:mo'o, da'am si e-da:ṣk i wam, e-we:gaj i ñe:nhog cem ñei
Jewed̥ e-ce:k, ag me:k ka:c
Do:da'ag cu:cwua, wat mo:momk e-cu:c
U'us cu:cwua, wat ku'agi im iawua, kut ag am cem ñeido
Kap si'alig tagiod̥ i wo:po'ijid ge s-tota e-hewelig, heg hekaj g e-i:bdag wa'usidk na:to
Id na:nki oid tagiod̥ i wo:po'ijid ge s-wepegi e-hehewelig, heg hekaj g e-i:bdag wa'usidk na:to
Im hud̥uñig tagiod̥ i wo:po'ijid ge s-cu:ck e-hehewelig, heg hekaj g e-i:bdag wa'usidk na:to
Im ka:cim tagiod̥ i wo:po'ijid ge s-ta:tki e-hehewelig, heg hekaj g e-i:bdag e-wa'usidk na:to.

Thus I did, Elder Brother Shaman, on open ground laid himself down, on it lying, on it four days completed, on it really pressed and arose, around himself looked and tried to see
Land got put, distantly lay
Mountains stood [formerly by somebody], now rottenly stood
Trees stood, now firewood toppled, and that I tried to see
And there from the east he caused to run his white winds, by means of which his heart got moistened and finished
There from the north he caused to run his red winds, by means of which his heart got moistened and finished
There from the west he caused to run his black winds, by means of which his heart got moistened and finished
There from the south he caused to run his glossy winds, by means of which his heart got moistened and finished.

I

I wu:ṣañ
Am si keiṣ
Ko wa hebai da:kam ge s-ñiokam o'odham, nt ag i miabidahim, am si keiṣ, am ba'ic i ñ-keiṣ
Ka hebai da:kahm ge s-ma:kaiskam o'odham, nt ag i miabidahim, am si keiṣ, am ba'ic i ñ-keiṣ
Ka hebai da:kam ge siakam o'odham, nt ag i miabidahim, am si keiṣ, am ba'ic i ñ-keiṣ
Ka hebai da:kam g u'uwi s-cu-ma:cim ge s-cu-behidag, ge s-cu-cekidag, nt a 'am si keiṣ.

I

[I] set out;
Stepped;
And some place sat the talker man, I neared him, on him really stepped again stepped
And some place sat the shaman man, I neared him, on him really stepped again stepped
And some place sat the warrior man, I neared him, on him really stepped again stepped
And some place sat the knowing women good gatherer, good storer, on them really stepped.

II

K am ju:pin, am si'alig wui s-komalim ñ-hiaṣp
Ai s-kakais do:da'ag

II

And there sank, then eastwards thinly myself buried
Reached the rich mountains

E-ṣoṣon-ab e-wa:pawañ, mamtoḍkaj
e-wi'iwin
Kunt ag eḍa ab jijiwim, ñ-i:bdag
e-wa'osidahim
Ab ce:mo'o ge a'anim ki:ta
K ag eḍa ab ka:c g na:nko cu'ijig
Kun ag eḍa ab jijihim, ñ-i:bdag
e-duwalidahim.

III

Am ju:pin, am si'alig wui s-komalin
ñ-hiaṣp
Ai s-kakais do:da'ag
E-ṣoṣon ab e-wa:pawañ, mamtoḍkaj
e-wi'iwin
Kuñ heg eḍa ab jijiwim, ñ-i:bdag
e-wa'osidahim
Ab ce:mo'ohim ge taṣ ceṣajid
Ko wa wuḍ tonwuakuḍaj, wesko
s-heweligdag, wesko s-cewagidag
wesko s-baiyokadag, wesko
s-nahagiokadag, wesko
s-wa:kcu (mukdam) hogidag, wesko
s-gi'ig (i) twal hogidag
Kuñ ag eḍa ab tono
Ko wa wuḍ maowuakuḍaj, wesko
s-heweligdag, wesko s-cewagidag
wesko s-baiyokadag, wesko
s-nahagiokadag, wesko
s-wa:kcu (mukdam) hogidag, wesko
s-gi'ig (i) twal hogidag
Kuñ ag eḍa ab maowua
Ko ha wuḍ tonwuakuḍaj, wesko
s-heweligdag, wesko s-cewagidag
wesko s-baiyokadag, wesko
s-nahagiokadag, wesko
s-wa:kcu (mukdam) hogidag, wesko
s-gi'ig (i) twal hogidag
Kuñ ag eḍa ab tono
O ha wuḍ i wescu wuḍ maowuakuḍaj
wesko s-heweligdag, wesko
s-cewagidag, wesko s-baiyokadag
wesko s-wa:ku (mukdam) hogidag
wesko s-gi'ig (i) twal hogidag
Kuñ ag eḍa ab maowua
Ab ce:mo'o ge wi:gi koṣkam ma:kai
Wuicudk bijimk wuicudk dahiwua, k ab
ha'icukaj we:maj ñiok, k waha
iñ-a:gid.

At their bases they seeped, with water
plants were covered
In that I entered, my heart got
moistened
Reached the feathered house
In that lay various possessions
In that I entered, my heart got vitalized.

III

There sank, then eastwards thinly myself
buried
Reached the rich mountains
At their bases they seeped, with water
plants were covered
In that I entered, my heart got
moistened
Reached the sun rising place
And there was its kneeling place, all
windy, all cloudy, all beaded, all
earringed, all crane feathered, all
swallow feathered

In that I knelt
There was its grasping place, all windy
all cloudy, all beaded, all earringed
all crane feathered, all swallow
feathered

In that I grasped
There was its kneeling place, all windy
all cloudy, all beaded, all earringed
all crane feathered, all swallow
feathered

In that I knelt;
There was its last grasping place, all
windy, all cloudy, all beaded, all
earringed, all crane feathered, all
swallow feathered

In that I grasped
Reached the down-nested shaman
Approached it straight and circled and
approached it straight and sat, spoke
something, and then to me it he told.

IV

I wu:ṣañk
Am si keiṣ
Ko wa hebai da:kam ge s-ñiokam o'odham
Kunt a am si keiṣk i miabidahim
Ab ce:mo'o
Heg wakusij
S-e'am do:dk dahiwua
Ha'icu hugij
O'ogmadk ba
Uackid ton
Ṣoṣamadk i je:j
Ka am we:gaj g s-keg wiapo'oge'elgaj g s-keg cehiagaj
T ag am pi iñ-huwij(id)
Ha'akia ab ka:cim na:nko cu'idag—ge'e bi'hugstalig, ge'e kustalig, ge'e hewostalig, ge'e ṣel wuitalig
Ha'akia ab ka:cim na:nko cu'idag pi in-huwijid i si kawijkad, kant ag da(dge).

IV

Set out and
Stepped
Someplace sat the talker man

I really took a step and neared him
Arrived
His mat
Deftly doing [I] sat [on it]
His food
Mixed with tears [I] swallowed
[His] cigarette
Mixed with snot [I] smoked
All around [were] his good boys, good girls
He didn't keep them from me
Various lasting possessions—hungriness thirstiness, coldness, straight shooting
Various lasting possessions he didn't keep from me and gathered them, so I wrestled [them].

V

I wu:ṣañk
Am si keiṣ
Ko wa hebai da:kam ge s-ma:kaiskam o'odham
Kunt a am si keiṣk i miabidahim
Ab ce:mo'o
Keg wakusij
S-e'am do:dk dahiwua
Ha'icu hugij
O'ogmadk ba
Uackid ton
Ṣoṣamadk i je:j
Ka am we:gaj s-keg wiapo'oge'elgaj g s-keg cehiagaj
T ag am pi iñ-huwij(id)
Ha'akia ab ka:cim na:nko cu'idag, ge'e bihugstalig, ge'e kustalig, ge'e hewostalig, ge'e ṣel wuitalig
Ha'akia ab ka:cim na:nko cuidag pi iñ-huwijidk i si kawijkad, kant ag da(dge).

V

Set out and
Stepped
Someplace sat the shaman man

I really took a step and neared him
Arrived
His mat
Deftly doing [I] sat
His food
Mixed with tears [I] swallowed
[His] cigarette
Mixed with snot [I] smoked
All around [were] his good boys, good girls
He didn't keep them from me
Various lasting possessions—hungriness thirstiness, coldness, straight shooting
Various lasting possessions he didn't keep from me and gathered them, so I wrestled [them].

VI

K i wu:ṣañk
Am si keiṣ
To hebai da:kam ge siakam o'odham
Kunt a am si keiṣk i miabidahim
Ab ce:mo'o
Keg wakusij
S-e'am do:dk dahiwua
Ha'icu hugij
O'ogmadk ba
Uackid ton
Ṣoṣamadk i je:j
Ka am we:gaj g s-keg wiapo'oge'elgaj g s-keg cehiagaj
T ag am pi iñ-huwij (id)
Ha'akia ab ka:cim na:nko cu'idag, ge'e bihugstalig, ge'e kustalig, ge'e hewostalig, ge'e ṣel wuitalig
Ha'akia ab ka:cim na:nko cu'idag pi iñ-huwijidk i si kawijkad, kant ag da (dge).

VI

And set out and
Stepped
Someplace sat the warrior man
I really rook a step and neared him
Arrived
His mat
Deftly doing [I] sat
His food
Mixed with tears [I] swallowed
[His] cigarette
Mixed with snot [I] smoked
All around [were] his good boys, good girls
He didn't keep them from me
Various lasting possessions—hungriness thirstiness, coldness, straight shooting
Various lasting possessions he didn't keep from me and gathered them, so I wrestled [them].

VII

I wu:ṣañk
I oi s-e eḍaoso ka:cim wo:git (a)
Ko wa in ka:cim tagio wo:gita, ge s-keg baiyoka s-hupidagk ag hugidag s-keg nanhagio s-hupidag ag hugidag
Kuñ ag ab si maopim, hekaj g ñ-i:bdag wa'usidk na:to
Ko wa in t-na:nki oid tagio wo:gita, ge u:s hickas ge s-cukudas, c hiosidas c hugid (ag), a'an gi'adag, wi:gi gi'adag ag hugid (ag)
O wa k im ha'ap hu ge s-paḍ o ḍ g ñ-elida (g), kuñ ag ab si hu:pañahim, si wanck (wu) ahim si kupal wuihim, si kehijundahim
S-ha'apk o hems a'i elidk taccu, na:nko ñ-i:mig (i).

VII

Set out and
Followed the center-lying road
There was a southern road, well beaded on the side, well earringed on the side
And I grasped it, used it to moisten my heart and finished
There was a northern road, cut wood blackened, and flowered sided, wing feather bowstring, down feather bowstring sided
On that side [north] bad were my thoughts, and I really uprooted it really broke it, really threw it down really stamped on it
Thus you may wish and plan, various kinsmen.

Ten days typically elapsed between the giving of the I'itoi speech and the departure of the war parties. These days included preparations of the sort that Mr. Lopez describes. According to Underhill and Gunst there were nightly meetings at the village round house where counting sticks were broken or thrown down each day, e.g., ten sticks in ten days. No more formal oratory was given until the parties met on their way to the enemy.

JOURNEY TO THE ENEMY

In the Lopez account the journey to the enemy required one day and one night—but the party made four stops. Perhaps this was standard in raids against 'straw' enemies. When the enemies were real, the journey surely varied, but a day and a night were probably the minimum. The night would be as important as the day. Not only was dawn the preferred time for the attack, but the night, at least the first night, was filled with ceremonies.

A fire was built. Speeches were given both of the sermonizing kind that Mr. Lopez describes and of oratory such as we give below. The custom according to Underhill and Gunst was for a number of orators to take turns while grasping a lance that had been set upright beside the fire. The oratory was followed by the singing and dancing that Lopez vividly describes. During this portion of the night, medicine men divined the location of the enemy and worked to render them defenseless, again as Lopez vividly describes.

Such ceremonies imply an enemy at a distance. The problem would be in finding them. If the party felt itself in danger, it would do the opposite: travel stealthily in the night and lie at rest hidden in the day. Perhaps Papagos did that too, but it is not stressed in the accounts.

The speech from this phase of the campaign is called the 'finished counters speech', so named because it was given on the night after the war parties departed, that is, on the night after the last of the counting sticks of the preparation period had been knocked down. Its preface mentions this fact.[2] It is a good study in oratory. In terms more concrete than most speeches it describes a war party's journey to the enemy including their camping places, their food, and their nights of ceremony. In its way it covers the same ground as the first half of Mr. Lopez' narrative. As an oration, however, it has a single hero throughout and it builds its story around his travels. There is nothing in the creation story to tell us who this hero was. The story in this case is extraordinarily complex, involving 'grown boys' (i.e., warriors), the sun, and the enemy. The translators are not sure that they have them all straight.

FINISHED COUNTERS SPEECH

Juan Gregorio, Santa Rosa

I ha'ap ant a wa'i do:da, u:s ñ-mulina, wesk aba'i wuidahim, ta ip e-ce:mo'ok ha ip e-ce:mo'o.	Thus I did, sticks I broke, all were given out, they [warriors] have gathered and finally gathered.

[2]It is not the only speech that might be given on the warpath. Examples of others, including a Pima version of this one, are found in Russell's *The Pima Indians*, 1908: 352-389.

Going on the warpath. Drawing by Mike Chiago.

meḍ has cu'igkam
ı ka:c, iya ha'icu paḍ
e-gegusid, ṣu:ḍagi
j b e-wawñic o wa iya ka:c.

ıai bṣ ga:mua.

ʋud mehedam ñ-ku:dag.
:bbehimk wa:ṣac al hiat ab
:i g sia ju:kam ñ-cukagida
u'ama, e-hugid an

ab dahiwa.
'in ñ-ai g ñ-wiapo'oke'elga
maj nanko ab i cem
ı, ta s-ho:tka'in ñ-ma:sid.

Then from someplace ran :
my relative and here st.
something of my bad-t
ate, with water of my s
himself and here stayeı
And the sun almost set.

I

And I took my burning ray
Away carrying it until off a
place there fell my mig
darkness, on one side y
side ashy.
I sat on it and stayed sitting
Then quickly reached me r
with them many things
then quickly it dawned

II

Kunt a'i bei siwud mehedam ñ-ku:dag.
Gamai al o i bebbehimk wa:ṣan ce:ckikuḍ an ant ha wa ce:.
Kut a s-ho:tka'in ñ-ai g ñ-wiapo'oke'elga, kuñ ag we:maj gamai pi ha'ap am do:da, al al na:kc oimmeḍdam, al ki:kc da:kam, al a'anc da'adam, gamai pi na:to'im hab ju:.
Wa:ṣan meḍadk eḍa at ha ha wa gei g sia ju:kam ñ-cukagida, e-hugid an u'ama, e-hugid an ma:tai.
Kunt ag da:m ab u'apa, kunt a ab ha'akia ñ-mu'a do'iyudk ba:.
We:cium taccu b s-ta:tkim gewsim, ta s-ho:tka'in ñ-ma:sid.

II

And I took my burning rays torch.
Away carrying it until off at a camping place I set it down.
Then quickly reached me my grown boys, with them mistreating the little earred running things, little house sitters, little feathered fliers, there were too many to do.
Farther on at the river there fell my mighty doing darkness, on one side yellow, on one side ashy.
On that I brought it [torch?], and many of my killings raw I ate.
Ahead desiring, throwing feelings, then quickly it dawned for me.

III

Kunt a'i bei siwud mehedam ñ-ku:dag.
Gamai al o i bebbehimk wa:ṣan ce:ckikuḍ an ant ha wa ce:.
Kut a s-ho:tka'in ñ-ai g ñ-wiapo'oke'elga, kut a ab ṣaṣk im huḍuñig wui wo:pk wa:ṣan s-u'upadag an wopoṣañ ga:ghai b e-ho'ihulikamk wa:ṣac al e-wapto kikijig baṣo b e-wo'inogidk wa:ṣac al hodait ab we:sk ab ha ha wa hehe'ejelwa.

At ha'ap ep ṣaṣkhim t-nanki oid wui wo:pk wa:ṣan s-u'upadag am wipi'iṣañ ga:ghai ab e-kokdahimk wa:ṣac al utko dadak baṣo ip e-wo'inogidk wa:ṣac al hodai dahak we:sk ab at ha wa namkidk na:to.

III

And I took my burning rays torch.
Away carrying until off at a camping place I set it down.
Then quickly reached me my grown boys, they grabbed and westward ran, there at the catclaw trees washes they ran across getting stuck with stickers, beyond in front of the sun shade doors they turned back and beyond at the little rocks they all skidded to a stop.
This way they also grabbed and northward ran, there at the catclaw trees tiny washes they crossed trying to kill and beyond in front of where the soapweed sits they turned back and beyond where the rock sits they all met again and finished.

IV

Kunt has i ṣulcudk i wu:ṣ hascu paḍ we:m.
Gam hu cem al s-cu:cu'igam si ta:tkhim, Kunt ag oidk gamai bṣ pi ha'ap am do:da, ge'eged mo:mim ñ-hemajkuḍ, cu:ck ba:bhaikam ñ-hemajkuḍ, to:ta wo:pkam ñ-wipckuḍ, gamai pi na:to'im hab ju:.

IV

I straight away departed with something ugly.
Off there little things touching I continued and beyond that mistreated my big earred people, my black tailed people, my white bellied food, there were too many to do.

Wa:ṣac al wapkt ab at ha wa gei g sia ju:kam ñ-cukagida, e-hugid an u'ama, e-hugid an ma:tai.
Kunt ag da:m ab u'apa, kant a ab ha'akia ñ-mu'a do'iyudk ba:.
We:cium̃ taccu b s-ta:tkim gewsim, ta s-ho:tka'in ñ-ma:sid.

V

Kunt a'i bei siwud mehedam ñ-ku:dag.
Gamai al o i bebbehimk wa:ṣan ce:ckikuḍ an ant ha wa ce:.
Kut a s-ho:tka'in ñ-ai g ñ-wiapo'oke'elga, kut kia am hu ñ-ba'ic g jeweḍ al s-kapaijim ñ-bihagidk na:to.
Kunt ag oidk gamai bṣ pi ha'ap do:da, ge'eged mo:mim ñ-hemajkuḍ, cu:ck ba:bhaikam ñ-hemajkuḍ, to:ta wo:pkam ñ-wipckuḍ, gamai pi na:to'im hab ju:.
Wa:ṣac al ko:m weco al ṣonaj ab at ha wa gei sia ju:kam ñ-cukagida, e-hugid an u'ama, e-hugid an ma:tai.
Kunt ag da:m ab u'apa, kant ha'akia ñ-mu'a do'iyudk ba:.
We:cium taccu b s-ta:tkim gewsim, ta s-ho:tka'in ñ-ma:sid.
Kunt a'i wu:ṣad g n-wiapo'oke'elga, ge ba'ag koṣ tagyo tu'ak na:to.

Ka ab ka:c ge ba'ag kos p si wui uliñc ñeiḍc o wa ab ka:.
Kunt a'i wu:ṣad g ñ-wiapo'oke'elga, ge ṣu:dagi wu:ṣdag tagyo tu'ak na:to.

Ka ab ge ṣu:dagi wu:ṣdag p si wui uliñc ñeidc o wa ab ka:.

Bañ ha wa i kaij, "Kut has e-ju:?"
"Jeweḍ ka:cim dodolim̃ ka:c, hodai da:kam dodolim daha, u:s ke:kam dodolim ke:k, ge'e ha'icu wo:pokc oimmeḍdam dodolim o oimmeḍ."

Bañ ha wa i kaij, "Kut has e-ju:?"
"Oig o we:sk ab kakiocud g ñ-wiapo'oke'elga, kuñ ke:kk hi ha'icu a:g."

Farther on at the bamboo there fell my mighty doing darkness, on one side yellow, on one side ashy.
On that I brought it, many of my killings raw I ate.
Ahead desiring throwing feelings, then quickly it dawned for me.

V

And I took my burning rays torch.
Away carrying it until off at a camping place I set it down.
Then quickly reached me my grown boys, there in front of me at the mounded earth they encircled me and finished.
I continued and beyond mistreated my big earred people, my black tailed people, my white bellied food, there were too many to do.

Farther on below at the hack berry tree's base there fell my mighty doing darkness, on one side yellow, on one side ashy.
On that I brought it, and many of my killings raw I ate.
Ahead desiring throwing feelings, then quickly it dawned for me.
Then I took out my grown boys, in the eagle nest direction put them and finished.
There lay the eagle nest facing them and they looked and listened.
Then I took out my grown boys, in the ocean coming out place put them and finished.
There lay the ocean coming out place facing them and they looked and listened.
I said, "What happened?"
"The lying earth peacefully lies, the sitting rock peacefully sits, the standing tree peacefully stands, the furry running-around-thing peacefully runs around."
I said, "What happened?"
"Go and put on all your legs, my grown boys, and here I stand and tell something."

At ha aṇ a we:sk ab kakiocudk ka wuḍ si s-e'eḍaoso ka:cim wo:g, kunt ag oidk am ha-cu:cia ge s-cu:ca'ajimakam g ñ-wipiop, kut ha am we:cium gi'ik ab ṣoṣk at a i at na:nko wa ha wa in ñ-a:g.

They all put their legs on and there was the center lying road, I followed it and stood up the tall ones of my boys, and they took four starts and many different things to me they told.

"S-wo:poik da:m g wo:pog mu'ipa, wa'i e-to:ta da:m s-wecijkam ma:s," bo wa kaij.

"On the bushy place the trails are many lying on each other they look fresh," they said.

"Aheu'u, at noḍa, al e-uwidag s-we:mam, e-alidag s-we:mam, ha'icu e-cu'idag s-we:mam," bañ a kaij.

"Yes, he's dizzy, his sister he wants to be with, his child he wants to be with, his possessions he wants to be with," I said.

Am ha-cu:cia ge s-cu:ca'ajimakam g ñ-wipiop, ta am we:cium gi'ik ab ṣoṣk at a i at na:nko wa in ñ-a:g.

There I stood up the tall ones of my boys, they took four starts and many different things to me they told.

"S-wo:poik da:m g ha'icu behiyupkuḍ s-wecijkam ma:s," bo wa kaij.

"On the bushy place the thing they have gathered looks fresh," they said.

"Aheu'u, at noḍa, al e-uwidag s-we:mam, e-alidag s-we:mam, ha'icu e-cu'idag s-we:mam," bañ a kaij.

"Yes, he's dizzy, his sister he wants to be with, his child he wants to be with, his possessions he wants to be with," I said.

Am ha-cu:cia ge s-cu:ca'ajimakam g ñ-wipiop, ta am we:cium gi'ik ab ṣoṣk at a i at na:nko wa ha wa in ñ-a:g.

There I stood up the tall ones of my boys, they took four starts and many different things to me they told.

"S-wo:poik da:m g ha'icu behiyupkuḍ s-wecijkam ma:s, go:kho o ḍ ki am o e-cu:cuḍ we:m at ki ia mo:t," bo wa kaij.

"On the bushy place the thing they have gathered looks fresh, twice with his nephew he loaded it," they said.

"Aheu'u, at noḍa, al e-uwidag s-we:mam, e-alidag s-we:mam, ha'icu e-cu'idag s-we:mam," bañ a kaij.

"Yes, he's dizzy, his sister he wants to be with, his child he wants to be with, his possessions he wants to be with," I said.

Am ha-cu:cia ge s-cu:ca'ajimakam g ñ-wipiop, gam hu a cem gi'ik ab ṣoṣk, he'es cuhugam eḍa t-wui juṣal juwiñhim, ta am a ṣa al pi ha cei, ta ia t-na:nko wa wa in ñ-a:g.

There I stood up the tall ones of my boys, then they took four starts, at midnight back to us they quietly tiptoed, they didn't speak out, then different things to us they told.

"O ob abṣ taṣo e-wuak pi we:gaj hodai daha," bo wa kaij.

"They are just in the open and not seated behind rocks," they said.

Kut kia g eḍa g ñ-wiapo'oke'elga, ge komagi wamaḍ cu:kug behik hemako hodai mo'ocudk a'i bañmeḍ.

There were my grown boys, grey snake the meat getter, and one of them hid in the rocks and crawled.

Kut kia g eḍa g ñ-wiapo'oke'elga, ge gewho s-cu-wiadkam cu:kug behik, hemako wi'iṣañ oidk a'i bañmeḍ.

There were my grown boys, gopher the good hunter meat getter, and one of them followed the little washes and crawled.

VI

At ag si'al abṣ ab i cem me:, kutt ag eḍa i
ñe:nk ab t-iawa.

T ab g ġ ñ-o:bga i wu:ṣañk cem ñeidogk
hejel e-waṣaiga keikonk im i iawa.

Ta an a bei g e-ciñkaj s-cu-muadkam,
k bekk im i ce:wim.
Tag ñ-o:bga i wu:ṣañ cem ñeidogk hejel
e-u:sga wañwank im i iawa.
Ta an a bei e-huckaj s-cu-muadkam,
k bekk im i ce:wim.
At ag taṣ apcut cem si sikol i me:, kutt ag
eḍa pi ha'icu dadagcudk a'i hugio.

S-ha'ap k hems a'i elidk taccu nanko
ñ-i:m.

VI

The morning started to run, and we
jumped and spilled ourselves [on the
Apaches].
Then my enemy got up and tried to see,
on his own grass he slipped and
spilled.
He who kills with his mouth grabbed
him, took him, and dragged him.
Then my enemy got up and tried to see,
on his own tree got torn and spilled.
Then he who kills with his claws grabbed
him, took him, and dragged him.
Then the sun was ready to rise, we had
nothing to wrestle and it was all
finished.
Thus you may wish and plan my various
relatives.

THE ATTACK

Mr. Lopez' full story of the attack is:

The sun shines
They like it
Well, and they kill them.

Such brevity concerning the climax of a ceremonial journey is common in Papago oratory as well as in prose. Whatever its cause, its effect is of extreme modesty. One can easily miss the part of a text which by Anglo-American standards should be its main point, as for example the mention of wine in a wine feast speech, the killing of the deer in a *ma'm'aga* speech, or the battle in a text on war. If the word 'kill' hadn't been used in the passage quoted above, we wouldn't have known that it was about an attack.

A much fuller account is given by Mr. Lopez of the selection of the men who would be killers. In recent years two men have been chosen on the night before the attack from the total of four participating villages. According to the author, his own selection came after the other three villages had been able to produce only one candidate. The choice finally came to his village, Santa Rosa, and with reluctance on his part, to him.

With this stress on individuals, one expects that the combat would be highly individual. All the accounts of Pima and Papago war confirm this. We should understand, however, that the individualism did not mean that peoples' actions were independent of group control. Quite the contrary. The individual combats were in full view of everyone and each man was intensely interested in what his companions would do. The successful raid was one in which, while little was said about it beforehand, there were no surprises as to who did what. The killers would kill and the modest people would stay back—but not too far. It is doubtful whether killers were agreed upon prior to attacks against real enemies, but something close to that may have been aspired to. This is why the medicine men worked to render the enemy helpless and why the leader kept the party under tight discipline. We note that in the 'finished counters' speech the hero, who was the leader of the expedition, gave orders continually and seemed to know which of his 'snakes' and 'gophers' would kill the enemy. The ideal was for people to act individualistically but in a completely predictable manner.

THE JOURNEY HOME

The killers are separated from the rest of the party. The rest return home as quickly as possible with the news of the successful raid and with the trophies that the killers have taken. These latter would be put on display, danced around, and returned to their takers after a period of celebration and purification.

The killers, having been separated, were put through a process that would make them *sisiakam*, 'heroes'. This process begins immediately after the raid and continues until the trophies are returned to them. The first step is to tie their hair into a bun and to provide them with scratching sticks. This is done by an already initiated *siakam*. He addresses them as *cu:cuḍ*, 'nephew', and they address him as *o:gta*, 'made father', the same terms as were used in the salt pilgrimage orations.

The acts of tying the hair and providing the scratching stick are accompanied by oratory. The speeches are given below. A third speech from this stage of the campaign is also given, namely a "speech on starting home." They are short speeches compared with those of the first phases of the warpath. They differ from those in another way as well: Rather than telling a story of what happened to a hero of long ago, they are concerned with what is being done to the hearer (the killer) at that moment. The latter difference is of emphasis, not of a wholly different manner of expression. In the hair tying and scratching stick speeches it is a question of beings coming to the enemy killer addressee—the idea of a journey is still there; in the starting home speech it is a question of a homeward journey as anticipated by the enemy killer.

BACK OF THE HEAD TYING

Juan Gregorio, Santa Rosa

Nañ a:ñi wuḍ m-o:gta c a:ñi ha'icu m-a:g?	Aren't I your made father and tell you something?
Na:gs si'alig ṣon ab ge s-u'am ñu:wi	It seems at the base of the east there is a yellow buzzard
Pṣ al ma:kai mo wa:g wuḍ m-o:gta	He's a little medicine man that is your made father
Heg amjeḍ i ji:wia	That's why he comes

Ha'icu m-a:g.
Napt s hemu i ma:s
Ha'icukaj ba:mk ṣoṣa
Ta am m-bekk am si m-da'ic
Ta am gei, ṣopol mu:kk i wamigk e-cegito.
Im huḍuñig wui i wuak cem ñeid
Kag da:m ab nagia g si cewajkam u'uhig
Ha'akia ab angew, kupt ag ṣa:gid s-i'omk da'iwuṣ.
Ka.cim tagio nagia g si cewajkam u'uhig
Ha'akia ab angew, kupt ag ṣa:gid s-i'omk da'iwuṣ.
Si'alig tagio nagia g si cewajkam u'uhig
Ha'akia ab angew, kupt ag ṣa:gid s-i'omk da'iwuṣ.
Ka wuḍ ge tokam hewel,
Nt ag i dagiu, hekaj si s-keg kawoḍk kuṣo om wu:,
Wi'ikamkaj si m-noipoṣadag.
Aheu'u, to wuḍ taccu, na:gs wuḍ m-taccu,
Kupt g oidk am nako g na:nko ta:hadkam.

He tells you something.
Aren't you newly born
With some kind of relationship crying
Then he took you and really threw you
Then [you] fell, were dead for a little while and came back to life.
To the west turned and looked
On it hung the very long bird
Several times flapping, between them you strongly jumped out.
In the south hung the very long bird
Several times flapping, between them you strongly jumped out.
In the east hung the very long bird
Several times flapping, between them you strongly jumped out.
And there is the little whirlwind,
I press it, with it nicely tie a knot on the neck,
With the remainder to bundle [?] you.
Yes, it is a desire, it seems like your desire,
Following that you feel the different kinds of feelings.

SCRATCHING STICK SPEECH

Juan Gregorio, Santa Rosa

Aheu'u, nañ a:ñi wuḍ m-o:gta
A:ñi ha'icu m-a:g.
Huḍuñig wui i e-wuak ñei g pi a'anam u'uhig
Mat wa:g wuḍ m-o:gta
Heg amjeḍ ji:wia
Ha'icu wo m-a:g.
K si mu'uk g macwidagk am si hu:p

Si e-hakkot
Si'alig wui i wo:po'ic.
Ta am ge s-cuhugam i e-wo'inok
Ta am ge s-keg noḍagigk s-keg naumdag

Hekaj s-keg kawoḍk kuṣo om wu:

U:s mu'ukat hemu si m-ke:ṣ.

Yes, aren't I your made father
I'm telling you something.
Towards the west [you] turn and see the featherless bird
That may be your new father
That's why he comes
He'll tell you something.
Very pointed medicine men's feathers he pulls out
Makes a ring from them
Eastward throws them.
Then the darkness returns
Then the good dizziness and good drunkenness
With it to nicely tie in a bunch on the neck
A sharp stick now sticks into you.

STARTING HOME SPEECH

Juan Gregorio, Santa Rosa

Do:wa'i, hekihu at a wa i himad g na:nko cu'igkam u'uhig da'adam, jewedo meddam.
Ha'as hebai wa i himdam wo:gita ka:cim, gamai ha-oidk ñeida.
Ka am daha g s-toha hodaik tag ab si e-keiṣ
Ba'ic daha g s-wegim hodaik tag ab si e-keiṣ
Ba'ic daha g s-cukam hodaik tag ab si e-keiṣ
Ba'ic daha g s-u'am hodaik tag ab si e-keiṣ
We:cim gi'ik ab ṣoṣk cem ñeid.

K ha'akia hohokimal hugidag, wa:g cecedop hugidag heg oidc cu'ijigc ñeidahim.
Ta'i hu m-oidc i med g tokam hewel, m-otko si wipic, kupt ag ta:tkc hab cu'ijigc ñeidahim.

Ka am wuḍ ke:kam u:s, hejel e:kdaj si:bañ, weco ab m-daṣwa.

Pi mia hebai ali m-ñeidam, a:gk hab o m-ju:
Pi mia hebai uwi, a:gk hab o m-ju:.

Aheu'u, to wuḍ ta:c, ha'as wuḍ m-ta:c, oig cem nako g na:nko ta:hadkam.

Ready, already have started the different kinds of flying birds and things that run on the earth.
For some distance a road is lying, [you] follow it and watch.
There sits a white rock and that gets stepped on
Farther sits a red rock and that gets stepped on
Farther sits a black rock and that gets stepped on
Farther sits a yellow rock and that gets stepped on
From there [you] take four stops and look.
Many butterflies by the side, many dragonflies by the side, along them [you are] going and looking.
From behind you starts to run a little whirlwind, on your back really twisting, and you feel it and are going and looking.
And there is a standing tree, in its own shadow sprinkling, under it they set you.
Not close any child will see you, that's why they do it to you
Not close any woman, that's why they do it to you.
Yes, it's a feeling, it seems like your feeling, you try to stand the different kinds of feelings.

PURIFICATION AND CELEBRATION

The final phase has two threads of activity, one centered on the *sisiakam*-to-be and one centered on everyone else. As the orations from this final phase of the rite are addressed only to the *sisiakam*, we will follow that thread first.

In Underhill's information, the heroes received a new set of 'made fathers' upon arriving in the vicinity of their village. These new ones would guide them through the final, purifying phase of their experience. By the time the heroes neared home, the new caretakers were waiting to establish them, with a speech, in a shelter or under a tree outside the village. According to Gunst, the 'made fathers' for the journey home were retained for the final phase; Mr. Lopez leaves the point moot.

The speech used at this point divides into *parts* as a normal oration, but as with the "starting home speech" of the previous phase, the hero is the warrior himself. The journey in this case is to a series of poles and trees, terminating at a 'standing tree' which no doubt represents the place away from the village where the 'made father' installs the hero.

Each day during his seclusion the initiate is visited by his 'made father'. The latter brings food consisting of a cup of water mixed with dried, ground corn (pinole). To show his fortitude the initiate drinks very little of this, for example he may drink only the liquid part off the top of the cup and throw away the thick part at the bottom. A speech given below, 'water drinking', pertains to these visits. This short speech says nothing about the hunger, thirst, and loneliness that the initiate would be experiencing. Rather it focuses on the dizziness and drunkenness that were thought to be within the liquid, and on the winds and 'hearts' (or 'spirits'—the Papago word *i:bdag* can be translated either way) that could be seen reflected in it. It is during this time that the men might have dreams or visions and learn songs.

SPEECH ON ESTABLISHING SIAKAM IN HIS SHELTER

Juan Gregorio, Santa Rosa

I

Pt o wa da'iwuñ
Am we:c gi'ik ab ṣoṣk cem ñeid
Ka wa cem ba'ic g go:k gikyo e-wui cu:ciak
Baṣo ab nagia g pi o'ohodkam kawaḍ
Sikoli bijimhim, eḍa p betañ
U:s ṣopolig baṣo nagia
Am eḍa kowoñ
Pt ag weco go:k huḍuñ.

II

I wu:ṣ
Am we:c gi'ik ab ṣoṣk cem ñeid
Ka wa cem ba'ic g waikk gikyo e-wui cu:ciak
Baṣo ab nagia g pi o'ohodkam kawaḍ
Sikoli bijimhim, eḍa betañ
U:s ṣopolig baso nagia
Am eḍa kowoñ
Pt ag weco go:k huḍuñ.

I

You will spring out
There ahead make four stops and look
There in front two poles are towards each other standing
In front there stands an unpainted shield
Turning around, thundering inside itself
A short stick hangs in front of that
Inside itself rustling
Below that you spend two nights.

II

Come out
There ahead make four stops and look
There in front three poles are towards each other standing
In front there stands an unpainted shield
Turning around, thundering inside itself
A short stick hangs in front of that
Inside itself rustling
Below that you spend two nights.

III

I wu:ṣ
Am we:c gi'ik ab ṣoṣk cem ñeid
Ka wa cem ba'ic ke:k g s-cehedagi
hahagkam u:s
Ta am we:c gi'ik ab ṣoṣk cem ñeid
Ga'i hu t-da:m ke:k g ñiokdam u:s
Weco ab ke:k g uacki ton
Hejel kucṣañ
Ka ab ki'ick wamṣ.

III

Come out
There ahead make four stops and look
There in front stands a green leaved tree

There ahead make four stops and look
There in the sky stands the talking tree
Below it stands a cigarette joint
By itself burning
[You] bite it and wet it.

IV

S-kuiwodam i:bhei
Ta wa:ṣ hu si ku:kugwa g s-to:ta
hahagkam u:s
Ta am we:c gi'ik ab ṣoṣk cem ñeid
Ka am wuḍ ke:kam u:s
Hejel e:kdag si:bañ
Tag weco ab m-daṣwa
Pi mia hebai ali m-ñeidam
Pi mia hebai uwi m-ñeidam, a:gk hab o
m-ju:.
Aheu'u, to wuḍ ta:c, ha'as wuḍ m-ta:c,
oig cem nako g na:nko ta:hadkam.

IV

Westward [you] breathe
There far stretches a white leaved tree

There ahead make four stops and look
And there will be a standing tree
Sprinkling in its own shade
Below that they will set you
Not close any child will see you
Not close any woman will see you, that's
why they do it to you.
Yes, it's a feeling, it seems like your
feeling, you try to stand the different
kinds of feelings.

WATER DRINKING SPEECH

Juan Gregorio, Santa Rosa

Ko wa wuḍ s-tondam ñ-wasib o wa iya
ka:c
Eḍa noḍagig e-mu'umk naumdag si:sk

I wo i hu t-da:m a'agṣp cu:cim sisiwulig

Ge juḍum i:bdag, ge ba'ag i:bdag, ge
wiṣag i:bdag
Hewel ta ha'akia i:ya si hemapi e-ul
ñ-wasib eḍa
Pt hemu io ba:.

There was my shining drink that here lies

Inside it dizziness sparkles [?] and
drunkenness sizzles
There above us are the upside down
standing whirlwinds
The bear heart, the eagle heart, the hawk
heart
Several winds here gather in my serving

You now will swallow it.

The final speeches of the *gidahim* come at the end of the purification period. This period might last four or fifteen or sixteen days and nights. On the final night the trophy takers are moved to the place where the rest of the people have been celebrating. Two speeches are recorded from this night. One of them recalls the actions taken by medicine men against the enemy—'Thus I mistreated my enemy'. As such it seems to belong more to the oratory spoken enroute to the enemy than to the oratory used in this final phase.

The second and final speech is a much longer one which was delivered at the time the new *siakam* was doused with cold water by his 'made father'. It is called the 'cure speech' as this final phase of the *gidahim* served as a cure for the heroes. In addition to the water dousing, the *sisiakam* were 'blown over' as Mr. Lopez explains. The Papago word *wusot* means 'to blow' or 'to cure'. The speech takes its hero through a series of strange and forbidding places. It starts with a reference to him as the creator of a world. To his surprise a 'bitter wind' comes from the west to destroy his creation. Afterwards he journeys to the underworld (which is how we interpret the reference to 'the land on the other side'), into the sky, and finally back to earth again at a fly's behest. There the hero seeks and finds enemies to kill. With statements such as 'Ready, man, now tell me straight and soon will appear my sin', this is one of the most psychological and the most perplexing of ritual orations. The hero finds himself a killer for reasons that he confesses he doesn't understand. The narrated events, while clearly ancient or "mythical" in character, have no place in any known version of the creation story. We will return to this speech below.

WAR PURIFICATION SPEECH

Juan Gregorio, Santa Rosa

Ha'ap ant a wa i do:da g ñ-o:bga
Mu'i na:nko cu'ijigkaj da:mai
  ce:kidahim
Kokoicudahim, kokosidahim
Ha'ap ant a wa i do:da g ñ-o:bga.
Ha'ap ant a wa i do:da g ñ-o:bga
Wepo cu'igkam we:maj oimmelidaj
  we:maj ñiokimadaj s-o:hodacud,
Kokoicudahim, kokosidahim.
Ha'ap ant a wa i do:da g ñ-o:bga
Alidaj komkidaj, s-o:hodacud
Uwigaj we:maj wo'imadag, s-o:hodacud

Kokoicudahim, kokosidahim, aheu'u.
T ab si'alig tagiojeḍ i himc g s-tondam
  ñ-bihagakuḍ
I himcudk oimmeligaj hugid an da:ṣk

Ha'ap i do:da.
T-nanki oid tagiojeḍ i himc g s-wegium
  ñ-bihagakuḍ

Thus I mistreated my enemy
Many different troubles putting on him

Making him sick, making him sleepy
Thus I mistreated my enemy.
Thus I mistreated my enemy
His companion-in-going-around's talking
  to him, make him hate
Making him sick, making him sleepy.
Thus I mistreated my enemy
Holding his child, make him hate
Lying together with his woman, make
  him hate
Making him sick, making him sleepy, yes.
From the east started my white wrapping
  up thing
Started and beside his favorite walking
  places it was set
Thus mistreating him.
From the north started my red wrapping
  up thing

I himcudk oimmeligaj hugid am da:ṣk

Ha'ap i do:da.
Im huḍuñig tagiojeḍ i himc g s-cuhuñ ñ-bihagakuḍ
I himcudk oimmeligaj hugid am da:ṣk

Ha'ap i do:da.
Ka:cim tagiojeḍ i himc g s-ta:tk ñ-bihagakuḍ
I himcudk oimmeligaj hugid ab da:sk

Ha'ap i do:da.
Ka wuḍ ha'icu cu'idaj

Nt a am u:g am ñ-da:m si ñe:nc
Ta ab si'alig tagiojeḍ g s-to:tam jejegos i wo:p
Huḍuñig tagiojeḍ g s-cuckam jejegos i wo:p
Heg we:m ab a'ai gegokiwa
Kuñ ag wepco si wa'usim bebbehim

Hascu ali ñ-behi
Uwi ñ-behi pi si ha:m e-ju:
I:ya ce:mo'o g ñ-jeweḍgak heg keiṣk im ke:kiwa
Heg daiṣk im dahiwa.
Ha'ap ko hems a'i elidk taccua na:nko ñ-i:m.

Started and beside his favorite walking places it was set
Thus mistreating him.
From the west started my black wrapping up thing
Started and beside his favorite walking places it was set
Thus mistreating him.
From the south started my glossy wrapping up thing
Started and beside his favorite walking places it was set
Thus mistreating him.
And there was something of his properties
High there above me I threw them
Then from the east the white dust storms ran
From the west the black dust storms ran

Together on both sides they stood
And I below them was wetly collecting things
Whatever baby I collected
Woman I collected, it wasn't hard to do
Here [I] arrived at my land and stepped and stood
Squatted and sat.
Thus you may wish and plan, my various relatives.

CURE SPEECH

Juan Gregorio, Santa Rosa

Aheu'u, ḍo oḍ hab ju:?
Kunt o wa a:ñi jeweḍ ce:k na:to
Da:m do:da'ag cu:cuia'ak na:to
Da:m u:s ke:ṣk na:to
Da:m ṣoṣongam ṣuṣugi to:ta'ak na:to
Da:m hemajkamcudk na:to.
A:ñi hebai hugkam am cem si ñeidcko g ñ-elid.
At a koi he'es o ta waṣan i hoi huḍuñig ṣon an ge siw hewel

Yes, who did it?
It is I, earth put down and finished
On top, mountains stood up and finished
On top, trees stood up and finished
On top, spring waters laid and finished
On top, people made and finished.
I for a long time will watch it, I thought.

Then after a while there moved at the base of the west the bitter wind

At a amjeḍ i meḍk u:s ke:kam i hu:pañk
hekaj i kokdahim, at a id oidk i hab
juccuhimk at a im hu daṣwa

Ab upam ha'ahogi i e-wuak cem ñeid.
Ka pi hebai u:s ke:k, pi hebai hemajkam
oimmeḍ.

From there it ran and standing trees
uprooted to use for killing, along it
went and was doing and away off it
stopped
It turned itself around and looked
Nowhere a tree stood, nowhere a person
moved.

I

Ko ha im ha'ap ka:cim jeweḍ s-ap am
ta:hadag
Kunt ag da:m ab wu:ṣ
To:ta ñ-ṣaṣpad dagk wu:ṣ
Ñ-gegkio s-cu'ucuwidk ab s-hiosigk wu:ṣ

Ñ-kua weco gi:kiok wu:ṣ

Ku'ukced ga:t dagk wu:ṣ
S-u'umaiskam dagk wu:ṣ
Kawaḍ ñ-holiwkad wu:ṣ
U:s mo'okam dagk wu:ṣ
We:sko s-heweligc wu:ṣ
We:sko s-cewagigc wu:ṣ
Ñ-wuiho ga'agkodk ñ-o'ohonk wu:ṣ.
Ko ha im ha'ap ka:cim jeweḍ s-ap am
ta:hadag
Kunt ag oidk gi'ik ab ce:ka
Ta am a ñ-ai g s-je'eckam u'uhigk
ñ-'iajidk kuhu.
Kunt ag ha-e:bidk ṣoṣak am noḍ
At a koi he'es kunt a upam jiwia
Kant heg hekaj am haha i si wa:mkaj an
ta:t.

I

The land on the other side felt fine

And on it I came out
My white shoes took and came out
My shoulder blades flowered and came
out
Below my forehead wrapped and came
out
Bent bow took and came out
Arrow took and came out
My rolled up shield and came out
Headed stick took and came out
All windy and came out
All cloudy and came out
My face zigzag painted and came out.
The land on the other side felt fine

Along it I took four steps
Then they reached me, the many birds,
and crowded me and hooted.
And I feared them and cried and turned
Soon reached home again
And because of that felt very strongly.

(Parts II and III are identical with Part I.)

IV

Ko ha im ha'ap ka:cim jeweḍ s-ap am
ta:hadag
Kunt ag da:m ab wu:ṣ
To:ta ñ-ṣaṣpad dagk wu:ṣ
Ñ-gegkio s-cu'ucuwidk ab s-hiosigk wu:ṣ

Ñ-kua weco gi:kiok wu:ṣ

Ku'ukced ga:t dagt wu:ṣ
S-u'umaiskam dagk wu:ṣ

IV

The land on the other side felt fine

And on it I came out
My white shoes took and came out
My shoulder blades flowered and came
out
Below my forehead wrapped and came
out
Bent bow took and came out
Arrow took and came out

Kawaḍ ñ-holiwkad wu:ṣ
U:s mo'okam dagk wu:ṣ
We:sko s-heweligc wu:ṣ
We:sko s-cewagigc wu:ṣ
Ñ-wuiho ga'agkodk ñ-o'ohonk wu:ṣ.
Ko ha im ha'ap ka:cim jeweḍ s-ap am ta:hadag
Kunt ag oidk gi'ik ab ce:ka
Ka ha'apjeḍ g aki ab ka:c
Ha'apjeḍ g wi'isañ ab ka:c
C heg we:m am e-meliew.
O wag ṣa:gid ab nagia u:s matdag
O wag ku:gt ab nagia cioj sisiwuda
O wa'ap bahid amjeḍ g ṣu:dagi ab akimeḍ, t heg ab ṃaowa, heg hekaj g am iñ-da:dagk o haha wa iñ-'a:g
"Do:wai, cu:cuḍ, ce:mo'oñ g m-o:gta," b at a cei.

My rolled up shield and came out
Headed stick took and came out
All windy and came out
All cloudy and came out
My face zigzag painted and came out.
The land on the other side felt fine

Along it I took four steps
From one side a big wash lay
From one side a little wash lay
And together there they met.
Between them hung a split stick
At its point hung a man's feather
From its tail the water ran, he touched it with it he rubbed me and then told me
"It's done, nephew, now get to your made father," he said.

V

Kunt a am wui cem gi'ik ab ṣoṣk cem ñeid
Ka wa:ṣac ge kapañ ṣu:dagi ka:c, o ag eḍa 'ab daha, "kup ki sai ju:kam ñ-o:gta," kunt ag wui am ceka

Ta'i hu e-wui i ñeidok o wa hab kaij
"Ṣa:pt cu'i ciojk hab e-juñhim, ko o wa s-ñ-e:bid g o'odham c pi heḍa'i ia s-ji:wima," b at cei
Ta ab cu:kugaj oid g e:'ed s-ka'akwoḍk daḍiwa, tag ab maowa, heg hekaj g am i ñ-da:dagk o haha wa iñ-a:g
"Do:wai, cu:cuḍ ce:mo'oñ g m-o:gta," b at a cei.

V

And I made four stops and looked
There the slapping water lay, there he sat, "You must be the great doer my made father," and towards him I stepped
Soon he saw it and spoke
"What kind of man are you to do this, since the people fear me and nobody wants to come here," he said
Along his body blood in little balls sat, he touched it, with it he rubbed me and then he told me
"It's done, nephew, now get to your made father," he said.

VI

Kunt a am wui cem gi'ik ab ṣoṣk cem ñeid
Ka wa:ṣac ge a'ai s-muk ṣu:dagi ka:c, o wa g eḍa ab daha, "Kup ki sai ju:kam ñ-o:gta," kunt ag wui am ceka
Ta'i hu e-wui i ñeidok o wa hab kaij
"Ṣa:pt cu'i ciojk hab e-juñhim, ko o wa s-ñ-e:bid g o'odham c pi heḍai ia s-ji:wima," b at a cei
Ta ab cu:kugaj oid g ṣu:dagi s-ka'akwoḍk daḍiwa, tag ab maowa, heg hekaj g am iñ-da:dagk o haha wa iñ-a:g

VI

And I made four stops and looked
There the sharp ended water lay, there he sat, "You must be the great doer my made father," and towards him I stepped
Soon he saw it and spoke
"What kind of man are you to do this, since the people fear me and nobody wants to come here," he said
Along his body the water in little balls sat, he touched it, with it he rubbed me and then told me

"Do:wai, cu:cuḍ, ce:mo'oñ g m-o:gta,"
   b at a cei.

VII

Kunt a am wui cem gi'ik ab ṣoṣk cem
   ñeid
Ka wa:ṣ hu ñ-ba'ic ge waik gikyo e-wui
   cu:c
O wa ki: nolk an daḍha wepeg toton,
   'a'al u'uwi, paḍ oks si:ki hupṣa sa
   woponam
At a ab cu:kugaj oidk heg e:'ed
   s-ka'akwoḍk daḍiwa, tag ab maowa,
   heg hekaj g am i ñ-da:dagk o haha
   wa iñ-a:g
"Do:wai, cu:cuḍ, ce:mo'oñ g m-o:gta,"
   b at a cei.

VIII

Kunt wui cem gi'ik ab ṣoṣk am ke:kiwak
   cem ñeid
Ta i hu ñ-da:mjeḍ i huḍuñ g s-tondam
   wo:gidak
Ab iñ ab ku:gwa
Kunt a ab a ha si keiṣk i oidk
Ant a in hu a'ahe da:m a:jim baṣo
Ce'ul gegewtpakc g cu:kug ab hehelig

Huawi e'elidag ha'hakia ab i da:m holiw
Huawi ba:bhai e:'ed p ṣo:gi
Mañ ag am haha cem si hega'icud
Ku kia g eḍa pi wuḍ hegai
Kut a i hu ñ-oidjeḍ i kaidag g s-cehedagi
   mu:wali ñ-ṣoiga, k at a im hu
   ñ-a'ahek o haha hab kaij
"Ṣa:pt cu'i ciojk hab e-wuac oimmeḍ,
   gama'i a'al, u'uwi, i:wagi t-e:sidk
   heg gamai wo:po'oc, na:nko kaidam
   t-hehemsdahim, ṣoṣagdahim," b at
   a cei.

IX

Kunt a'ab haha si keiṣk i 'oidk ant a im
   hu a'ahe
A:ñ a hab kaij

"It's done, nephew, now get to your made
   father," he said.

VII

And I made four stops and looked

There in front of me the three poles
   together stood
There at the house top were sitting the
   red ants, children women, ugly old
   lady deer antler hats
Along his body the blood in little balls
   sat, he touched it with it he rubbed
   me and then told me

"It's done, nephew, now get to your made
   father," he said.

VIII

And I made four stops and stood and
   looked
There from above me came down the
   shining road and
At me it stopped
I stepped on it and followed and
There reached the sky's front
Willows were cut and meat was on them
   spread out
Deer skins several had been folded
Deer tails bloody bundled
Perhaps then I will really use this
But no, this can't be it
Then from behind me sounded the green
   fly my pet, from behind it overtook
   me and then spoke
"What kind of man are you and do and
   wander, back there the children,
   women, and young girls, they [the
   enemies] steal them from us and
   away they run, with their different
   sounding laughing and crying,"
   he said.

IX

Then I really stepped and continued and
   arrived back there
I said

"Do: wai, cioj, oig ṣeliñ ñ-a: gidk oi a hab
ma: s'in g ñ-cu'ijig," b ant a cei
Ka hab kaij
"Heu'u, in wa'i a'aligc in o wa'i u'uwi,
kutp hebaijeḍk hab a e-ju:," b at
a cei.

"Ready, man, now tell me straight and
soon will appear my sin," I said
And he said
"Yes, here there are children and here
there are women, it must be from
someplace else that it happened,"
he said.

X

Kunt a an ha-we: gaj i da'iwuṣ
Ka jeweḍ s-moikc ka: c
Kunt ag oidk an i cem je: kckahimk abṣ
hab iñ-melinoki
A: ñ a hab kaij
"Do: wa'i, cioj, oig seliñ ñ-a: gidk oi a hab
ma: s'in g ñ-cu'ijig. Nañ gahijeḍ
m-oid? ṣelijeḍ añ m-oid, kaṣ i: ya
amam," b ant a cei

Ka hab kaij
"Heu'u, wa: ṣ heg i a: gk heg we: nad i
hab t-ju: nan," b at a cei
Kunt a'ap haha i kokda, kokdak and
haha wa i hugio.
S-ha ampk o hems a'i elidk taccu, na: nko
ñ-i: m.

X

And I behind them jumped out
The earth softly lay
I continued and tried to track them and
just only met myself
I spoke
"Ready, man, now tell me straight and
soon will appear my sin. Am I
following you sideways? Straight I'm
following you, this must be the
place," I said
And he said
"Yes, go ahead and tell it and together we
can die," he said
And then I was killing them, killing
them, and then I finished it.
Thus you may wish and plan, my various
relatives.

We turn now to the other thread of the final phase of the *gidahim*, the celebration. The enemy trophies are tied on a pole and carried home by the bulk of the war party. When close to home, the returning party is met by old women from the village who take the trophy pole and dance with it. Younger women also arrive to sing and dance with the weapons of the returning warriors. Underhill was told that a payment was required to retrieve the weapons from the young women.

Underhill and Gunst differ slightly on the events that follow the return. Both accounts are probably correct and simply represent variations in the methods of celebrating. Both speak of a category of dance songs called *limhu ñe'i* ('limhu song'—the *limhu* is untranslatable). According to Underhill, this type of song was used inside the village starting at sundown during each of the nights of the heroes' seclusion. She states that the singing took place around the trophy pole which had been fixed in the ground.

According to Gunst, the *limhu* songs were used only during the first day's festivities as the returning warriors, old ladies, and young women made their triumphant entry into the village: "Every few feet (as the party made its way to the village) dances called 'limos' were executed (p. 33)." To Gunst, the songs used for the nightly celebrations in the village were not *limhu* songs, but were cycles which belong to a general category of celebrating of "social dancing" songs. Among these might be 'swallow songs', 'woodpecker songs', 'hummingbird songs', 'eagle songs', 'wind songs', and 'lightning songs'. Such cycles are dreamed by individuals and can run into hundreds of items. They could be used at many occasions besides war victories, such as rodeos, fiestas, and school dedicatons.

Comparing the two accounts, we see a common outline for the first day and subsequent nights of celebrating, but differences in the song types as well as in the specifically warlike nature of the celebrating:

Early in the day of the war party's return, old women and young girls sing and dance while holding war trophies and weapons. Through the day of the party's return, *limhu* songs are used to accompany the party into the village (Gunst); or a meeting is held at the round house to plan for an intervillage celebration at the end of the heroes' seclusion (Underhill). Through the nights of the heroes' seclusion, the celebrating consists of social dancing and celebration songs—with no handling of trophies or weapons (Gunst); or the celebrating consists of *limhu* songs and dancing around the trophy pole erected in front of the round house (Underhill).

It may be added that according to Gunst only four nights were spent in celebration or seclusion while according to Underhill it was a fifteen night period. Whichever account is followed, it appears that the four or fifteen nights were less directly concerned with war than was any other time period of the entire *gidahim*. The trophy takers were in seclusion and the trophies themselves, if present (as in Underhill's version), were simply sung around, not handled directly.

Mr. Lopez agrees with Gunst. In his account *limhu* songs, accompanied by a rattle, are sung through the day of the heroes' return. At this time old women take the stick with the scalp—he calls it a 'rag'—and dance with it. At sundown the celebrators go home to eat. When they return in the darkness of the first night of the heroes' seclusion, they sing and dance to a different type of song. The songs are accompanied by scraping on a basket. They would be the "social dancing" songs of Gunst's account.

A night long celebration called *wulida* ('the tying') culminates the war campaign. It was held on the night following the sixteenth day of seclusion according to Underhill, or on the night following the fifth day according to Gunst and Lopez. It featured a special kind of song called *kumuda ñe'i* ('smoking song') and a special kind of dancing called *kapaḍwa* ('war dance' or 'leaping dance'). Again our sources differ as to who sang the songs, to whom they were sung, and where the *kapaḍwa* dancing fit in; but again they agree on the general outline of the event.

This outline has a part of the night taken over by *kapaḍwa* dancing, in which weapons are again handled; part of the night given over to 'blowing' on and dousing the heroes (now returned to the main group) with cold water; and a climactic event at dawn when the trophies are tied into bundles for the heroes to keep—hence the name *wulida*.

According to Gunst the *kumuda* songs had more to do with the war dancing aspect of the ceremony than with the 'blowing' and washing aspect. According to Underhill it was the opposite: There was first the *kapaḍwa* dance around the trophy pole, complete with brandishing weapons, then came a long process of singing *kumuda* songs over, blowing over, orating over, and pouring water over the heroes.

In this case Mr. Lopez agrees with Underhill. First there is the *kapaḍwa;* then comes the singing, in twos, of another type of song—these would be the *kumuda* songs these singers 'blow' over the heroes. Finally comes the dousing with water and an accompanying speech.

The accounts agree that the warriors were kept at some distance from the fire and trophy pole around which the *kapaḍwa* dancing was done. They stress that the heroes sat motionless while the war dancers cavorted; they suffered cold while the dancers kept warm, their weapons were at rest while the other warriors' weapons were flourished.

Finally, Underhill and Gunst agree that the dawn ceremony of 'tying' the trophy was analogous to baptizing a baby. After the first rays of the rising sun struck it, the trophy was closed in a basket, cradled in the arms, addressed as 'my child' by the trophy taker and his wife, and as 'younger brother' by the couple's children. (Mr. Lopez does not speak of this.) With this welcoming of a captured enemy spirit into Papago society, the war campaign was closed.

TWO SPEECHES ON MADE FATHERS

Because the speech is so perplexing, let us draw certain parallels between the 'cure speech' and the Anegam type "B" salt pilgrimage speech. We hope for a clearer understanding of the relation between "power" and "purification." These are the two texts in the collection that speak extensively about 'made fathers' who, as we know, are the men who in real life oversee the purification of the *sisiakam*. It is not clear whether individuals bearing that title worked also in the salt purification. As Underhill and Brennan describe it, the work in that rite could have been done by 'blowers' *(s-wusos o'odham)* and 'medicine men' *(mamakai)* rather than 'made fathers'.[3]

Viewing the speeches as stories, it is first noted that they have a westward orientation, notwithstanding the dominant orientation of Papago warfare to the east.[4] This orientation is expressed in the 'cure speech', first, by the direction from which the destructive 'bitter wind' came. The same wind, but not in destructive form, is mentioned in the Anegam speech, where it is associated with Coyote's 'land' beyond the ocean and with war implements. Second, we can read the hero's itinerary as passing through the underworld, and we understand that

3. 'Made father' is a special status. One can be a 'blower' for a *siakam* and not stand in the special relation of 'made father' to him.

4. The Pimas fought in three directions, with the Apaches to the east, the Yavapais to the north, and the Yumans to the west. Papago warfare seems to have been mostly with the Apaches.

the underworld is entered at the place where the sun sets west of the ocean shore. This interpretation is inferential, resting on the phrase 'the land on the other side' and on a corroborating passage in a version of the 'I'itoi speech' different from the one discussed in this book (Bahr, 1975:99-101). Third, we would associate the various 'waters' of the Anegam speech, which are decisively located in the west, with the waters visited by the hero in the 'cure speech'. At these waters the heroes of both speeches meet their 'made fathers'.

Now the point on power grants and purifications is that the same act may be either one or the other. In other words, these two concepts which "sound different" in English appear quite closely related in Papago culture. The Anegam speech is ostensively about power grants, but it includes various physical ministrations onto or into the hero's body. The 'cure speech' is ostensively about purification, but it includes some of the very same acts, notably the 'made father's' pressing of blood and water onto the hero. As the speech is delivered, we understand that the *siakam*'s actual 'made father' douses him with cold water. We would call the act, as done in the ritual, a washing off, a form of purification; we would call the act as narrated in the speech, a putting on, a form of power grant. They are very close.

Continuing with the plot of the two speeches, the point at which their stories diverge is after the episodes with the 'made fathers'. At this point the hero in the Anegam speech has what he wants and he goes home. The hero of the 'cure speech' ascends into the sky, finds something that he doesn't want, and is called back to earth to engage in killing. Difficult though this sequence is to grasp psychologically, it proves the point on power and purification. The hero did his killing after the encounters with 'made fathers'. The washings with blood and water were preparations for killing, not cleansings after it.

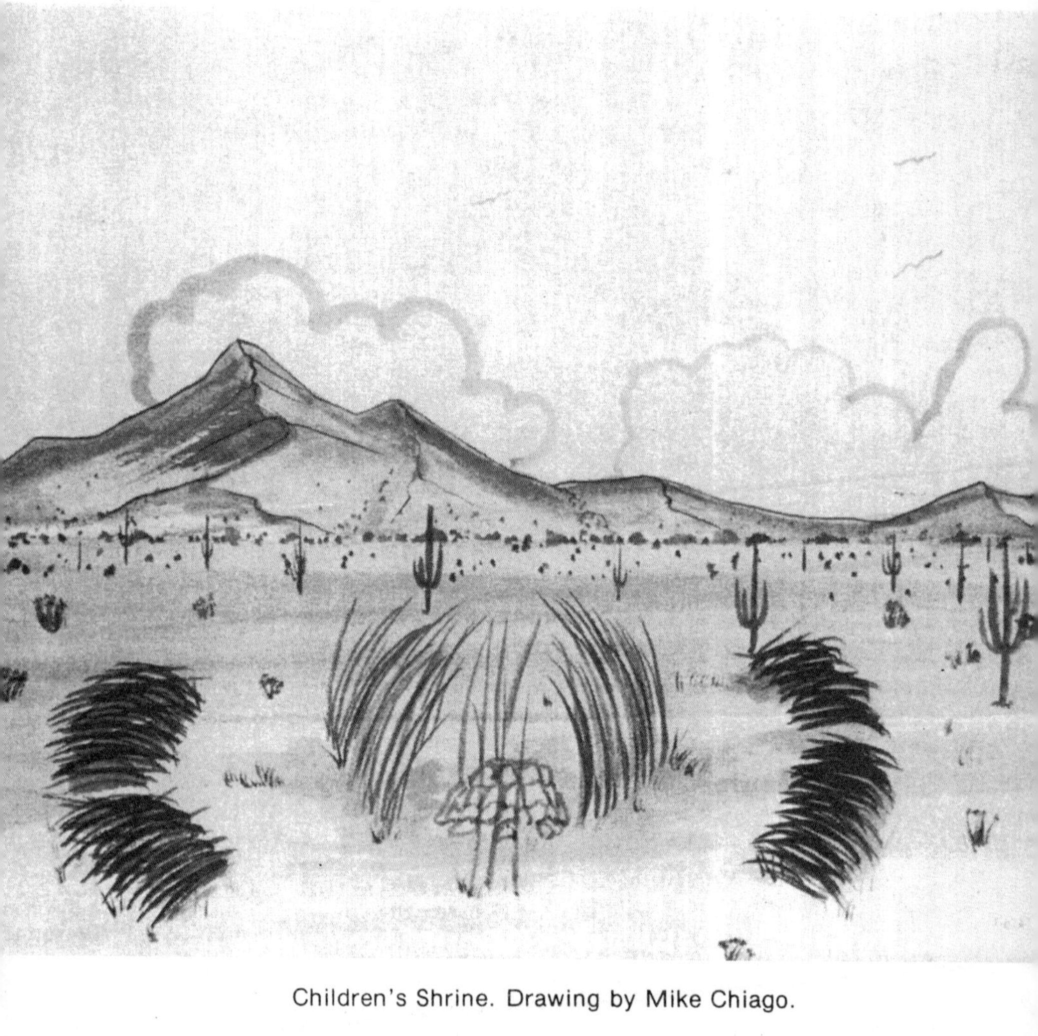

Children's Shrine. Drawing by Mike Chiago.

Flood

West of Santa Rosa is a shrine well known to most Pimas and Papagos, where it is said that four children were sacrificed in ancient times to stop a flood. The children are believed to be still alive beneath the ground. People visit the shrine to ask favors of them and to leave offerings at any time of year, but every two years a formal visit is paid to them by representatives of Santa Rosa, Ak Chin, Anegam, and Ge Aji (Sil Nagia). This is to renew the shrine. It is done in April or May. While there is only one such shrine, other villages hold observances at the same time of year and for the same purpose, which is to anticipate the rainy season, then still two months away. We will try to see how these rites oppose the coming of the rains from the east with the ocean to the west.

The renewal of the shrine proceeds as follows: Men from each of the four villages journey to a nearby mountain to cut fresh green ocotillo branches. April-May is the season when this plant turns green. Ocotillos behave like saguaros only sooner. They "come to life" on their own accord at a time when the days are getting longer and hotter, and when the summer rains are still two months away. It is recalled that ocotillos were conceived as wet by nature in the oration for the *a'ada*.

Stripped of their leaves and pitchy bark, the branches are brought to the shrine and stood upright around its periphery like a fence. The ocotillos of the previous renewal, now gray and dry, are piled on two semicircular mounds, one to the south and one to the north of the fence. These mounds have received the old ocotillos since the shrine was begun. No one knows how long this has been, but according to legend the shrine was built by the Hohokam, not the Papagos. In any case, the dirt at the base of the mounds is mixed with crumbled ocotillos. Pieces of ironwood, an extremely durable wood, are used in this rite as in the *ma'm'aga*. In this rite they are carved to represent squash and buried in the four directions at gaps left in the ocotillo fence. The ocotillos are called 'corn'. Next, the hole where the children were sacrificed is opened. A collection of beads and seashells is removed and cleaned. The offerings are returned to the hole with a few new items added. Finally tufts of eagle down are fastened on sticks and placed at the four directions.

Two speeches are used during the renewal, one after the cutting of the fresh ocotillo, the second after finishing the work at the shrine. They were recorded by Underhill from Jose Moreno of Santa Rosa.

SPEECH AT THE OCOTILLO CUTTING

Jose Moreno, Santa Rosa

Na:nko cu'igkam ñ-i:mig	Various relatives of mine
Ha'as atkam huñ em-wepogi	Broad bottomed corn in your likeness
Ha'as atkam ha:l em-wepogi	Broad bottomed squash in your likeness
Am o ge s-keg bai	There it will get nicely ripe
Hekaj am o ge s-kegkam huḍ	Therefore it will be a nice evening
K o om gamai has o i e-ju:, hebai ha'icu cem ha-ñia k o hu:.	Later on it will happen, someplace you will ask for food and eat.

SPEECH ON COMPLETING THE RENEWAL (TO THE EAST, SOUTH, AND NORTH)

Jose Moreno, Santa Rosa

S-ap i m-do:da ñ-si:s	Well you were treated, my elder brother [or sister]
Hemu i:ya m-ke:ṣ g t-iagta	Here stand before you our offerings
Hemu i o ñeiyopa	Now you will come out
Gamai wo wo:p, wo ce:mo'o si'aligc eḍ	Run over there, reach the east [south, north]
Gam hu wa'aki eḍa ha'icu bahidag ab hab cu'ig	There in the rainhouse are ripe things
Hu:ñ bahidag, ha:l bahidag, bawi bahidag, we:s ha'icu am hugkam bahidag	Ripe corn, ripe squash, ripe beans, everything is ripe
Wenog ab o bei, pi si ham ju:	There you will get it, it won't be difficult
I o u'apa, ṣo'ig t-jeweḍ da:m	Bring it here, on our poor earth
T ag am o ñei.	That will be seen.

(TO THE WEST — lines four through six)

Gamai wo wo:p, wo ce:mo'o huḍuñigc eḍ	Run over there, reach the west
Gam hu wa'aki eḍa g ha'icu bahidag ab hab cu'ig	There in the rainhouse are ripe things
Ṣu'uwat bahidag, da:pk bahidag, opon bahidag	Ripe *ṣu'uwat*, ripe *da:pk*, ripe *opon* [all wild grasses or greens]

The first speech apparently is addressed to the men who have done the cutting. It tells them that they may now go away, that they will ask for food at a later time, and then they may eat. It is not clear whether the speech means tonight, at their homes, or tomorrow, at the shrine, or even some later time. On another level and considering the speech to follow, one might view it as being addressed to the sacrificed children.

The second speech is unlike most of the orations in this book in that it is addressed to a specific spiritual or supernatural audience—the children. It implores this audience to do something. They are to go to rainhouses in the four directions and bring back ripe crops.

We have seen how rainhouses figure in the wine feast and salt pilgrimage orations. A difference between the shrine speeches and those others is that the reference here is to bringing back ripe crops. The reference in the other speeches was to obtaining winds and clouds. After the rain, according to the other speeches, seeds sprout and form thick stemmed, big leaved, plants. It is generally not said where the seeds would come from. Presumably the hosts had them. (One speech, the Anegam type "A", says that the hero received seeds from a rainhouse.) That ripe crops are requested in the shrine speech may or may not be significant. It sounds as if the granting of this wish would make farming unnecessary. What is significant is that the flood children are sent to rainhouses and not to the ocean, the underworld, or to any other place. As we would expect from the earlier chapters, the western rainhouse has a special status. Where the other rainhouses have crops, the western one has only wild food; it is non-agricultural.

Children's Shrine. Photo by Ruth M. Underhill, ca. 1933.

Following the renewal at the shrine, there is a night of singing 'basket scraping' songs at the village round house. These are songs about wind, rain, and crops. The purpose of the rite, Underhill was told, is good luck in farming. The speech to the children is the first official turning of thoughts towards the agricultural year that lies ahead.

Two other villages were found by Underhill to have observances similar to the shrine renewal at this time of year. They were Mesquite Root and Kaka. In each village the observance centered on bringing a sacred bundle into the village, opening it, perhaps renewing it, and singing 'scraping stick' songs. At Mesquite Root this was done at intervals through the spring as the cactus picking season drew nearer: when the saguaros budded, when they flowered, when they had their first fruits, and immediately before picking. This custom shows a smooth transition from the ocotillo season celebrated by Santa Rosa and its neighbors, to the saguaro harvest. One could truly say for Mesquite Root that the entire two or three month process was one ritual, in other words that singing over the bundle marked the preparation phase for the saguaro picking journey which led finally to that village's 'sit and drink'. More, one can say that the "wet season" of the year starts with the ocotillos of April or May and runs to the *ma'm'agas* of fall or even until the November *wi:gita* of the northern villages.

At Kaka the bundle was opened to see whether its contents were wet or dry. If wet, it would be a rainy summer, if dry, not. A dance was held with two boy and two girl dancers who represent, Underhill thinks, the children sacrificed at the shrine (1946:75). The observance might be repeated as at Mesquite Root if the village headman felt that the summer might not be wet enough.

The spring rites anticipate the rains but they do so, at least in some villages, by recalling a flood. What does a flood have to do with rain? The rains of summer come mostly from the southeast. To meteological science, they are monsoons born over the Gulf of Mexico. Let us quote an excellent account on the subject:

> "During the second half of June upper level moisture begins to move into Arizona from the Gulf of Mexico. For a few weeks it alternately advances and retreats, much like an ocean tide. After the first week of July, however, it is fairly well established. Then it is augmented at lower levels by periodic surges of moist tropical air from the Pacific Ocean that push up the Gulf of California. These surges often generate long, arching squall lines, with haboobs (dust storms—*jegos* in Papago) fanning out below and ahead of each cell in the line....
> Satellite photographs have shown that storm systems of this type often develop south and east of Tucson from dense masses of clouds over the Sierra Madre Occidental of northern Sonora in Mexico. The cloud masses form almost explosively just after noon, starting out as isolated cells that move slowly northwest.... The systems generally intensify as they move up the Santa Cruz valley (from Tucson) to Phoenix (Idso, 1976:109-110)."

This is essentially a scientific version of the mockingbird speech. The "storm alley" that Idso describes from Tucson to Phoenix is the eastern side of the Papago reservation.

Prior to the coming of the Whites, Papagos did not know about the Gulf of Mexico. Their knowledge of geography to the east of them stopped with the Sierra Madres of northern Sonora. Their ocean was to the west, the Gulf of California, in the opposite direction from whence the storms come. They knew the particulars of that ocean well from the salt pilgrimages.

The ocean is salty; its water is different from that which falls from clouds. There is almost no vegetation at the seashore that they visited. As one travels westward to the Gulf from Papago country he encouters drier and drier lands. It is recalled that a key point in the salt pilgrimage is a run up a 'Sandy Hill' or a 'Black Mountain', depending on the route. At this point or just before it, the journeyers cut their scratching sticks, no doubt because on the far side of the hill or mountain there will be no more wood. The vegetation along the ocean is confined to leathery shrubs. There are no trees. The beach itself is pure sand, the purest meeting place of water and matter. The water is salty, the matter is hard white and yellow particles of decomposed seashells. Entirely absent are fresh water and the dust, powder, and mud of "normal" soil. One has the exact opposite experience as he travels east from Papago country. This is the direction of increasingly lush vegtation. The trees change from mesquite to oak and pine. The closest pine forest is atop Mount Lemon, just north of Tucson and within sight of many Papago villages. In Papago it is called 'Frog Mountain.'

A final significant property of the ocean is that it stays. It is permanent water. This is in contrast to the sweet water that comes from summer rains. As Juan Gregorio expressed the ocean's permanence in another book:

> ...Look, I will explain something clearly,
> which is that the ocean lies over there,
> well, look, as for it (the ocean) something is quite apparent
> that it is there, and there it stays,
> and it never wanders.
> It just stays through the years
> for as long as it lies, that one (ocean)
> (Bahr, Gregorio, Lopez, and Alvarez, 1973:300-01).

It may be seen that the flood which was averted by the sacrifice of the children belongs to the "ocean" side of the water system. This is clear from at least one version of the story of the shrine's origin:

> In the spring of one very dry year a man chased an animal down a hole. He dug out some more dirt. And he put in his hand again to pull out whatever it was that he had seen go in there. Then there was a roaring noise.... The man sat there. The roaring came again. Then a strong wind came out of the hole. And the wind smelled like the ocean air (Wright, 1929, 187).

In short the ocean was threatening not to stay, but to flood the land. Brennan, of course, made exactly the same point at the beginning of his account of the salt pilgrimage. It may be noted that another very important flood of the creation story, which wasn't averted, originated in a baby's tears—also salty as anyone knows who has tasted tears. The concept of babies and children in all this we must leave as a loose end.[1] Let us consolidate what we have, namely that destructive floods are associated with salt water from the western ocean, in contrast to the "constructive" floods of fresh water from the predominantly eastern summer rains.

Correlated with the salt water flood is the 'bitter wind' mentioned in the salt pilgrimage type "B" and war ('cure') speeches. This wind has a basis in southern Arizona weather patterns. Dr. Idso (personal communication) states that extremely violent and large scale wind storms sometimes come from the west in the early spring. A storm of such violence would be unlikely from any other direction at that time of year. Characteristically such a storm carries no rain. Idso recalls one from 1972 whose dust blotted out the sun on a perfectly cloudless day. To him they do not smell of the sea.

We recall the 'cure speech's' description:

Then after a while there started to move at the base of the west the bitter wind
From there it ran and standing trees uprooted to use for killing, along it went and was doing and away off it stopped
It turned itself around and looked
Nowhere a tree stood, nowhere a person moved.

The likeness to the "real" storms is the absense of any redeeming rain. The same trait separates those storms from the summer rains. We may suppose if there were any rain with this kind of wind, according to the logic of the speeches, it would be salt water. We close with this contradictory dossier on the west: the source of violent dry winds, of soft, misty rains, and of threatened salt water floods. The last rite of the year—or should we say the first rite of the new one—is in reference to that.

[1] In his book, *Olmec Religion*, Karl Luckert discusses several Hopi stories which may be compared to the Papago legend of the childrens' shrine (1976: 159-65). The threat of a flood is involved in both cases. Luckert connects the Hopi stories with a broad, and he feels, ancient religious complex involving human sacrifice, serpents, and agriculture. His book is recommended to readers who would like to place the Papago materials in a broader context. While it cannot be said that the details of the Papago flood sacrifice are perfect matches either for the Hopi stories or the ancient serpent cult that may underlie such sacrifices, there is no doubt that Papago religion in general shares much with the Pueblos in the short run and with Mesoamerica in the long run. The reader may wish to compare the Papago wine feast, for example, with the Hopi snake dance. Both are meant to bring on the summer rains and both involve ritually induced vomiting; the fact that the Papagos use "wine" and the Hopis use an "emetic" may shed light both on Papago drinking and on Hopi medicine. Equally, one may ask whether some aspects of the serpent, which figures so prominently in Luckert's reconstruction of ancient Mesoamerican religion, have counterparts in the meanings that Papagos assign to saguaro cactuses and ocotillo. Such comparisons force one beyond the confines of his own thought categories. They are recommended to Indian readers interested in the oneness of Native American religions, and to non-Indians interested in testing the symbols of their own tradition (e.g., "serpent" and "sacrifice") against the multiplicity of another world.

References Cited

Alvarez, A., and K. Hale
1970 "Toward a Manual of Papago Grammar: Some Phonological Terms." *International Journal of American Linguistics* 36, no. 2, pp. 83-97.

Bahr, D.
1975 *Pima-Papago Ritual Oratory, A Study of Three Texts.* San Francisco, Indian Historian Press.

Bahr, D., J. Gregorio, D. Lopez, and A. Alvarez
1973 *Piman Shamanism and Staying Sickness (Ka:cim Mumkidag).* Tucson, University of Arizona Press.

Griffith, J.
1975 "The Folk-Catholic Chapels of the Papagueria." *Pioneer America* 7, no. 2, pp. 21-36.

Haefer, J.
1979 *O'odham Celkona* (The Papago Skipping Dance). In *Southwest Indian Ritual Drama,* ed. C. Frisbie. School of American Research Albuquerque, University of New Mexico Press.

Idso, S.
1976 "Dust Storms." *Scientific American* 235, no. 4, pp. 108-114.

Jones, R.
1971 "The Wi'igita of Achi and Quitobac." *The Kiva* 36, no. 4, pp. 1-29.

Joseph, A., R. Spicer, and J. Chesky
1949 *The Desert People.* Chicago, University of Chicago Press.

Luckert, K. W.
1976 *Olmec Religion, a Key to Middle America and Beyond.* Norman, University of Oklahoma Press.

Russell, F.
1908 *The Pima Indians.* Washington, D.C., Bureau of American Ethnology, Annual Report 26. Reedition 1974. Tucson, University of Arizona Press.

Saxton, D., and L. Saxton
1969 *Papago & Pima to English, English to Papago & Pima Dictionary.* Tucson, University of Arizona Press.
1973 *Legends and Lore of the Papago and Pima Indians.* Tucson, University of Arizona Press.

Spicer, E.
1962 *Cycles of Conquest.* Tucson, University of Arizona Press.

Underhill, R.
1936 *Autobiography of a Papago Woman.* Menasha, Wisc., American Anthropological Association Memoirs, no. 48.
1939 *Social Organization of the Papago Indians.* New York, Columbia University Contributions to Anthropology, no. 30.
1946 *Papago Indian Religion.* New York, Columbia University Press.

Wright, H.
1929 *Long Ago Told.* New York, Appleton.

Index